Praise for Thich Nhat Hanh

"He shows us the connection between personal, inner peace and peace on earth."
—His Holiness the Dalai Lama

"Thich Nhat Hanh is a real poet."
—Robert Lowell

"Thich Nhat Hanh writes with the voice of the Buddha."
—Sogyal Rinpoche

"Thich Nhat Hanh is more my brother than many who are nearer to me in race and nationality, because he and I see things the exact same way."
—Thomas Merton

(continued on next page . . .)

Praise for *Fragrant Palm Leaves*

"One of the sweetest and most personally revealing of Thich Nhat Hanh's books, it shows the planting of his seeds of remarkable wisdom."

—Jack Kornfield,
author of *A Path with Heart*

"Enlightening . . . To read his thoughts is to understand the connection between public life and private life, and that such 'interbeing' makes for ecstatic joy."

—Maxine Hong Kingston

"One of the greatest teachers of our time . . . In *Fragrant Palm Leaves*, the venerable poet emerges poignantly disclosing the essence of enlightenment, and also life itself!"

—Robert Thurman,
author of *Inner Revolution*

"Informative and inspiring."

—*Publishers Weekly*

GOING HOME

JESUS AND BUDDHA

AS BROTHERS

Thich Nhat Hanh

RIVERHEAD BOOKS
New York

Riverhead Books
Published by The Berkley Publishing Group
A division of Penguin Putnam Inc.
375 Hudson Street
New York, New York 10014

Copyright © 1999 by Thich Nhat Hanh
Book design by Deborah Kerner
Cover design by Jess Morphew

First Riverhead hardcover edition: September 1999
First Riverhead trade paperback edition: October 2000
Riverhead trade paperback ISBN: 1-57322-830-3

The Penguin Putnam Inc. World Wide Web site address is
http://www.penguinputnam.com

The Library of Congress has catalogued the
Riverhead hardcover edition as follows:

Nhat Hanh, Thich.
Going Home : Jesus and Buddha as brothers / Thich Nhat Hanh.
p.   cm.
ISBN 1-57322-145-7
1. Buddhism.   2. Christianity and other religions—Buddhism.
3. Buddhism—Relations—Christianity.   I. Title.
BQ4012.N43   1999   99-30519 CIP
294.3´372—dc21

PRINTED IN THE UNITED STATES OF AMERICA

10   9   8   7

CONTENTS

INTRODUCTION

At the beginning of the last great Ice Age, Neolithic artists created a series of extraordinary paintings deep inside the earth in the region of southwest France now known as the Dordogne. These masterworks may be the oldest-known expression of the human spirit. The land above these subterranean cathedrals is today rich and fertile, blessed not only with a hospitable climate, rich soil, and abundant water but also with a people who nurture the land. It is to their great credit that this region of France, unlike so much of the earth, is more fertile now than when the first Homo sapiens set foot here thirty thousand years ago.

Today, the region is primarily agricultural, supporting vineyards, plum orchards, and fields of sunflowers. Growing and eating good food is a way of life, a passion, and an art. Few tourists come to this remote region east of Bordeaux on their tour of la belle France, and fewer still explore the narrow roads and small villages. The people here do not yet move to the frantic pace of modern city life. They are still attuned to the natural rhythm of the sun and the seasons passing over the fields.

Located here in this cradle of humanity is a string of three small settlements, or hamlets, two of which are old farms, one a former youth hostel. The sign out front, faded and slightly askew, lets visitors know that they have arrived at Plum Village or, in French, Village des Pruniers. The buildings in Plum Village at first appear to be typical of the surrounding countryside. Built mostly of stone, they have stood for centuries as barns, farmhouses, tool sheds, and granaries. On closer examination, one sees that they are now being used as kitchens, dining rooms, classrooms, sleeping quarters, and meditation halls.

The walls, many of which were once plastered, have been stripped of all ornamentation, revealing the rocks, clay, and mud used to construct them centuries ago. Here the heaviness and richness of the earth itself is revealed. The windows are simple, the floors unfinished, and the heat often comes from wood burning in crude stoves fashioned from old barrels.

The dirt paths are lined with flowers, bamboo, and fruit trees. There are also small signs scattered here and there advising the walker to "breathe and smile," that "each moment is a wonderful moment," or that "peace is every step." The rustic beauty and charm of the place, however, does not account for the most remarkable characteristic of Plum Village—the deep quiet.

The quietness of Plum Village is more than the absence of noise. It is something else. It is truly peaceful here. People move slowly, smiles are contented, steps are deliberate, breaths deeper and longer. The land itself somehow seems softer, and the weather gentler even when it is cold. In late December, with the Atlantic Gulf Stream coming ashore on the coast only one hundred miles west, Plum Village tends to be very rainy. The paths become muddy, and the deep clay sticks to the soles of shoes. Outside of the main meditation hall, feet are caked with this red soil. The people awaiting entry huddle beneath umbrellas, searching for a dry spot to store their shoes. They enter the hall quickly, or as quickly as the pace of life in Plum Village allows, and find a chair or cushion upon which to sit.

The day has been cold and wet, but everyone is feeling warm. Christmas is one of the biggest festivals of the year in Plum Village, and, except for the summer retreat, it attracts the most visitors. The day began at 4:30 a.m. with meditation and chanting, just as in the Christian monasteries only a few miles away. Here in Plum Village, however, the chanting is not in Latin or French but rather in Vietnamese.

The monks and nuns assembled here are French, Thai, English, Irish, American, German, South African, Vietnamese, Japanese, and, most noticeably, Buddhist. For although this land has been a stronghold of Christianity for centuries, today it also supports a more ancient path. This day the songs and chants have come from both the Christian and the Buddhist traditions. In the early morning darkness, Christmas carols have been sung along with the daily litany of Buddhist sutras, gifts have been exchanged, and flowers have been laid at the altar to honor both the namesakes of Christianity and of Buddhism. Dinner, which has just ended, included traditional

Christmas dishes from all of the nationalities represented. Songs have been sung in a dozen different languages. Among the visitors to Plum Village this day are priests and nuns from the great Christian citadels of Ireland, France, and Italy. As people take their seats, about half on floor cushions in the classic cross-legged style of the East and half in plastic chairs being unstacked from the corner, two tall American Buddhist monks, one speaking softly in his Texas twang, work together to get the fire going in the old cracked stove.

Soon, Thây will arrive. Thây is the affectionate name given to The Venerable Thich Nhat Hanh, the founder of Plum Village. At seventy-two, Thây has lived an extraordinary life in an extraordinary time. Since the age of sixteen, he has been a Buddhist monk, living the life of an ascetic and seeker of the way. He has survived three wars, persecution and assassination attempts, and thirty-three years of exile. He is the master of a temple in Vietnam whose lineage goes back over two thousand years and indeed is traceable to the Buddha himself. He has also written more than one hundred books of poetry, fiction, and philosophy, founded universities and social service organizations, rescued boat people, led the Buddhist delegation at the Paris Peace Talks, and been nominated for the Nobel Peace Prize by Rev. Martin Luther King, Jr.

During his lifetime, Thây has also learned to know and love the West and its spiritual traditions. He is one of the greatest spiritual teachers alive today, and his message of Buddhist mindfulness has been embraced and become a part of Christendom. His altar now holds not only a picture of the Buddha, his traditional spiritual ancestor, but also of Jesus Christ.

When Thây walks through the door, everyone stands to greet him. He walks calmly, slowly, and deliberately to the small, rough podium set about two feet up off the floor. He carefully removes his coat and sits down. He then lifts the glass set before him with both hands and, with one fluid motion, raises it to his lips and drinks some of the warm tea. After setting down the glass, he looks up and brings his palms together in the classic Buddhist greeting. He bows, silently saying to himself, "I bow to you, an enlightened being to be."

The community bows a greeting in return, and, in a moment, a bell is rung. The sound is deep and long and pleasant. It rings in waves until finally the inviter of the bell places her hand gently on the rim and stops the reverberations. After another thoughtful pause, Thây, speaking in a very soft, sweet voice accented with Vietnamese and French, says, "Dear friends, today is December twenty-fourth . . ." And everyone in the room who hears this voice knows that Thich Nhat Hanh is indeed their dear friend.

—PRITAM SINGH
South Woodstock, Vermont

GOING HOME

JESUS AND BUDDHA

AS BROTHERS

ONE

THE BIRTH OF UNDERSTANDING

Dear friends, today is the twenty-fourth of December 1995. We are in the Lower Hamlet, in our Winter Retreat.

There are things that are available to us twenty-four hours a day. It depends on us to enjoy them. The fresh air is available to us twenty-four hours a day. The question is whether we have the time and awareness to enjoy it. We cannot blame the fresh air for not being there. We have to look back to see whether we take the opportunity and the time to be aware of the fresh air, and to enjoy it. One of the conditions that helps us be free to enjoy what is there is our mindfulness. If our mindfulness is not there, then nothing will be there. We will not be aware of the beautiful sunshine, the fresh air, the stars, the moon, the people, the animals, and the trees.

There is a French writer whose name is André Gide. He said that God is available to us twenty-four hours a day. God is happiness. God is peace. Why do we not enjoy God? Because we are not free. Our mind is not there. We have no capacity of touching God, or of enjoying Him or Her. The practice of mindfulness helps us to free ourselves to enjoy what is there.

TWO REALITIES

There are two levels of relationships. The first level is the relationship between us and other beings. In Christianity, we hear the expression "horizontal theology." This kind of theology helps us see and touch what is there around us. Horizontal theology helps us establish links with what is around us, including human beings, animals, vegetables, and minerals. Our daily practice should help us get in touch with these beings, animate or inanimate, because by getting in touch with them, we will be able to get in touch with God.

Getting in touch with God is symbolized by a vertical line and is called "vertical theology." These are the two dimensions. If you do not succeed in getting in touch with the horizontal dimension, you will not be able to get in touch with the vertical dimension. There is a relationship between the horizontal and the vertical. There is interbeing between the two. If you cannot love man, animals, and plants, I doubt that you can love God. The capacity for loving God depends on your capacity for loving humankind and other species.

THIS IS, BECAUSE THAT IS

Let us visualize the ocean with a multitude of waves. Imagine that we are a wave on the ocean, and surrounding us are many, many waves. If the wave looks deeply within herself, she will realize that her being there depends on the presence of all the other waves. Her coming up, her going down, and her being big or small depend entirely on how the other waves are. Looking into yourself, you touch the whole, you touch everything—you are conditioned by what is there around you.

In the teaching of the Buddha, we learn that "this is, because that is." "This is like this because that is like that." It's a very simple teaching but very deep. Because the other waves are, this wave is. Because the other waves are like that, this wave is like this. Touching yourself, you touch the whole. When you are capable of touching yourself deeply, and touching others deeply, you touch the other dimension, the dimension of the ultimate reality.

A wave is made of other waves. You can discover the relationship between that wave and all the other waves with the principle of cause and effect. But there is another level of relationship, and that is the relationship between the wave and the water. The wave is aware that she is made of the other waves, and at the same time she realizes that she is made of water too. It is very important for her to touch the water, the foundation of her being. She realizes that all the other waves are also made of water.

In Buddhism we speak of the world of phenomena *(dharmalakshana)*. You, me, the trees, the birds, squirrels, the creek, the air, the stars are all phenomena. There is a relationship between one phenomenon and another. If we observe things deeply, we will discover that one thing contains all the other things.

If you look deeply into a tree, you will discover that a tree is not only a tree. It is also a person. It is a cloud. It is the sunshine. It is the Earth. It is the animals and the minerals. The practice of looking deeply reveals to us that one thing is made up of all other things. One thing contains the whole cosmos.

When we hold a piece of bread to eat, if mindfulness is there, if the Holy Spirit is there, we can eat the bread in a way that will allow us to touch the whole cosmos deeply. A piece of bread contains the sunshine. That is not something difficult to see. Without sunshine, the piece of bread cannot be. A piece of bread contains a cloud. Without a cloud, the wheat cannot grow. So when you eat the piece of bread, you eat the cloud, you eat the sunshine, you eat the minerals, time, space, everything.

One thing contains everything. With the energy of mindfulness, we can see deeply. With the Holy Spirit, we can see deeply. Mindfulness is the energy of the Buddha. The Holy Spirit is the energy of God. They both have the capacity to make us present, fully alive, deeply understanding, and loving. That is why in our daily life, we should live mindfully, we should live with the Holy Spirit so we can live every moment of our daily life deeply. If we do not live each moment deeply, there is no way we can touch the ultimate dimension, the dimension of the noumena.

It seems as though the wave and the water are two different things, but in fact they are one. Without water, there would be no wave, and if we remove the wave, there is no water. There are two levels and two kinds of relationships. When we speak of cause and effect, we have to be aware on what level we are speaking. Is it on the level of phenomena or on the level of noumena? It is very important not to mix up the two.

In Asia, there are two schools of Buddhism, called the *Madhyamika* and the *Dharmalakshana*, that strongly stress the separate contemplation of the noumenal (the level of true nature), and the things that reveal themselves on the level of the phenomenal. The Madhyamika school teaches emptiness, *shunyata*, and the Dharmalakshana school teaches the phenomenal aspects of reality. The Dharmalakshana school encourages us to touch the world of the phenomenon, and the Madhyamika school helps us understand more deeply the world of the noumenal. The Madhyamika school encourages us to touch the water. The Dharmalakshana school encourages us to touch the waves. Both of them maintain that you should not mix up the relationship between one wave and another wave, and the relationship between the wave and water. You have to observe and contemplate the noumenal and the phenomenal separately. Of course there is a relationship between water and wave, but this relationship is very different from the relationship between waves and waves. This is very important. When we say this wave is made of all the other waves, we are dealing with the phenomenal world. We are speaking of causes and effects in terms of phenomena. But it's very different when we say that this wave is made of water. By separating the two relationships we will save a lot of time, ink, and saliva.

When you say that humankind was created by God, you are talking about the relationship between water and wave. God did not create man in the same way a carpenter creates a table. All our Christian friends would agree with that. The way God created the cosmos was quite different. You cannot mix up the two dimensions. You cannot consider God as one of the things that operates in the realm of phenomena. There are many theologians who are able to see this. Paul Tillich said that "God is the ground of being." The "ground of being" is the noumenal aspect of reality. God is not a being in the phenomenal world. He or She is the ground of all being. It would not be difficult for Christians and Buddhists to agree on this.

We can talk about the phenomenal world, but it is

very difficult to talk about the noumenal world. It is impossible to use our concepts and words to describe God. All the adjectives and nouns that we use to describe waves cannot be used to describe God. We can say that this wave is high or low, big or small, beautiful or ugly, has a beginning and an end. But all these notions cannot be applied to water. God is neither small nor big. God has no beginning or end. God is not more or less beautiful. All the ideas we use to describe the phenomenal world cannot be applied to God. So it's very wise not to say anything about God. To me the best theologian is the one who never speaks about God.

Not being able to speak about God does not mean that God is not available to us. I agree with André Gide who said, "God is available to us twenty-four hours a day." The question is whether you are touching God twenty-four hours a day. Perhaps you don't touch him at all during these twenty-four hours.

TOUCHING GOD, TOUCHING NIRVANA

In both the Christian and Buddhist practices, if you are not able to touch the phenomenal world deeply enough, it will be very difficult, or impossible, to touch the noumenal world—the ground of being. If you are aware that the fresh air is there, and if you can deeply touch and enjoy the fresh air, you have a chance to touch the *ground* of the fresh air. It's like the wave touching the water. The practice of touching things deeply on the horizontal level gives us the capacity to touch God—to touch the noumenal level or the vertical dimension.

We know that the wave is the water, and we know that the water is the ground of the wave. The wave suffers because she forgets this fundamental fact. When she compares herself to other waves, she suffers. She has anger, jealousy, and fear because she is unable to touch the ground of her being, which is water. If the wave is capable of deeply touching the water, her ground of being, she will transcend her fear, jealousy, and all kinds of suffering.

By touching this ultimate dimension, we get the greatest relief. We have to practice in our daily life so that we will be able to touch the ultimate. You can touch the ultimate when you drink a cup of tea or when you practice walking meditation. We can touch the noumenal world by touching the phenomenal world deeply.

In Buddhism, we speak of nirvana. We are not supposed to speak about nirvana because it is the level of the noumenal where all notions, concepts, and words are inadequate to describe it. The most we can say about nirvana is that it transcends all notions and concepts.

In the phenomenal world, we see that there is birth and death. There is coming and going, being and non-being. But in nirvana, which is the ground of being equivalent to God, there is no birth, no death, no coming, no going, no being, no non-being. All these concepts must be transcended.

Is it possible for us to touch nirvana? The fact is that you are nirvana. Nirvana is available to you twenty-four hours a day. It's like the wave and the water. You don't have to look for nirvana elsewhere or in the future. Because you are it. Nirvana is the ground of your being.

One of the ways to touch the world of no birth and no death is to touch the world of birth and death. Your own body contains nirvana. Your eyes, nose, tongue, body, and mind contain nirvana. If you go deeply into it, you touch the ground of your being. If you think that you can only touch God by abandoning everything in this world, I doubt that you will touch God. If you are seeking nirvana by rejecting everything that is in and around you, namely form, feelings, perceptions, mental formations, and consciousness, there is no way that you can touch nirvana. If you throw away all the waves, there will be no water for you to touch.

NOT A PERSON,
NOT LESS THAN A PERSON

The first principle we have to remember is that we should not mix up the phenomenal level with the noumenal level. We should not discuss nirvana or God in terms of phenomena. That would help save our time and energy. In discussing whether God is a person or not a person, you are trying to compare the ground of being with one expression at the phenomenal level. You are making a mistake. Why spend your time discussing whether God is a person or not, or whether nirvana is personal or impersonal?

Teilhard de Chardin, the French scientist and theologian, once said that the cosmos is deeply personal and personalizing, that it is in the process of personalizing all the time. He is caught in the conflict between personal and non-personal, which is a dualistic way of thinking. In his thinking is the assumption that there are two different things. One is the person, and the other is the non-person. It is the assumption that everything that is not a person is a non-person. That is the duality. That is what he got caught in. Whether God is a person or not a person, that is the question for many people. Theologians and others of us struggle to find the answer. We can save a lot of energy by recognizing that this is not useful at all, because we know that all concepts have to be transcended if we are to touch the ground of our being deeply.

When we ask, "Is God a person or is God not a person," we get lost. In fact, God is not a person, and God is not a non-person. There is a German theologian who expresses this very beautifully: "God is not a person, but not less than a person." It is a very Zen-like statement. Why do we have to imprison God in one of these two notions: person and non-person? Do you really need to define God like that?

In the Buddhist vision, there's no line separating the two. The person contains the non-person and the non-person contains the person. In Christianity, a lot of time and energy has been used to discuss whether or not God is a person. But in Buddhism that is not a big problem, because we know that a person is made of non-person elements and vice versa. When you look at a person you can see the non-person elements like animals and plants. When you look at a person you can already see the Buddha. You don't need the Buddha to manifest through your perception to recognize it as existing. Because you can already see the lemon in the lemon blossom.

If you are to penetrate deeply into reality, you have to get rid of notions. We can speak of the wave as high or low, beautiful or less beautiful, coming or going, being born or dying. But we cannot use these notions to speak about water. So why do we spend so much time and energy discussing whether God is a person or not?

BEYOND FORMS

The dialogue between Buddhism and Christianity has not gone very far, in my opinion, because we have not been able to set up a solid ground for such a dialogue. This is a reflection of the present situation:

Buddhists believe in reincarnation, the possibility for human beings to live several lives. In Buddhist circles, we do not use the word reincarnation very much: we use the word *rebirth*. After you die, you can be reborn and can have another life.

In Christianity, your life is unique, your only chance for salvation. If you spoil it, then you will never get salvation. You have only one life.

Buddhism teaches that there is non-self, *anatta*.

Christianity clearly teaches that a Christian is a personalist. Not only are you a person, a self, but God is a person, and He has a self.

The Buddhist teaching of emptiness and no substance sounds like the teaching of no being.

Christianity speaks of being, of existence. The teaching of St. Thomas Aquinas speaks of the philosophy of being, *la philosophie de l'être,* the confirmation that the world is.

There is compassion and loving-kindness in Buddhism, which many Christians believe to be different from the charity and love in Christianity. Charity has two aspects: your love directed to God, and your love directed to humankind. You have to learn how to love your enemy. Our Christian friends have a tendency to remind us that the motivation of love is different for Christians and Buddhists. There are theologians who say that Buddhists practice compassion just because they want liberation; that Buddhists don't really care about the suffering of people and other living beings; that they are only motivated by the desire to be liberated. In Christianity, your love is grounded in God. You love God, and because

God said that you must love your neighbor, so you love your neighbor. Your love of your neighbor springs from the ground of your love of God.

Many people, especially in Christian circles, say that there are things in common between Christianity and Buddhism. But many find that the philosophical foundations of Christianity and Buddhism are quite different. Buddhism teaches rebirth, many lives. Christianity teaches that only this one life is available to you. Buddhism teaches that there is no self, but in Christianity there is a real self. Buddhism teaches emptiness, no substance, while Christianity confirms the fact of existence. If the philosophical ground is so different, the practice of compassion and loving-kindness in Buddhism and of charity and love in Christianity is different. All that seems to be a very superficial way of seeing. If we have time and if we practice our own tradition well enough and deeply enough, we will see that these issues are not real.

First of all, there are many forms of Buddhism, many ways of understanding Buddhism. If you have one hundred people practicing Buddhism, you may have one hundred forms of Buddhism. The same is true in Christianity. If there are one hundred thousand people practicing Christianity, there may be one hundred thousand ways of understanding Christianity.

In Plum Village, where many people from different religious backgrounds come to practice, it is not difficult to see that sometimes a Buddhist recognizes a Christian as being more Buddhist than another Buddhist. I see a Buddhist, but the way he understands Buddhism is quite different from the way I do. However, when I look at a Christian, I see that the way he understands Christianity and practices love and charity is closer to the way I practice them than this man who is called a Buddhist.

The same thing is true in Christianity. From time to time, you feel that you are very far away from your Christian brother. You feel that the brother who practices in the Buddhist tradition is much closer to you as a Christian. So Buddhism is not Buddhism and Christianity is not Christianity. There are many forms of Buddhism and many ways of understanding Buddhism. There are many ways of understanding Christianity. Therefore, let us forget the idea that Christianity must be like this, and that Buddhism can only be like that.

We don't want to say that Buddhism is a kind of Christianity and Christianity is a kind of Buddhism. A mango cannot be an orange. I cannot accept the fact that a mango is an orange. They are two different things. We have to preserve the differences. It is nice to have differences. *Vive la différence.* But when you look deeply into the mango and into the orange, you see that although they are different, they are both fruits. If you analyze the mango and the orange deeply enough, you will see the same elements are in both, like the sunshine, the clouds, the sugar, and the acid. If you spend time looking deeply enough, you will discover that the only difference between them lies in the degree, in the emphasis. At first you see the differences between the orange and the mango. But if you look a little deeper, you discover many things in common. In the orange you find acid and sugar, which are in the mango too. Even two oranges taste different; one can be very sour and one can be very sweet.

LOOKING DEEPLY:
MINDFULNESS AND
THE PRESENCE OF GOD

Our Christian and Jewish friends like to speak about doing everything in our daily lives in the presence of God. You light a candle, you eat your meal, you embrace your child, you talk to your neighbor, you do everything in your daily life as if God is listening to you, looking at you, and is aware of your actions. You do everything in the presence of God.

The word *mindfulness* is not used in Christian and Jewish circles because mindfulness is a Buddhist word. But what is mindfulness? Mindfulness is to be aware of everything you do every day. Mindfulness is a kind of light that shines upon all your thoughts, all your feelings, all your actions, and all your words. Mindfulness is the Buddha. Mindfulness is the equivalent of the Holy Spirit, the energy of God.

THE SURVIVAL
OF POSSIBILITY

Let us look at the nature of impermanence. I don't think that our Christian friends ignore the impermanent nature of things. You are born, you grow up, and you change every day in terms of body, feelings, perceptions, mental formations, and consciousness. When you are five years old, you are different from when you were two years old—not only in terms of the body but also in terms of feelings, perceptions, and so on. Everything is changing.

Not only is the physical changing but also your mind is changing. This observation leads you to the insight that there is no permanent entity that you can call *yourself.* Nothing among the five elements by which we identify ourselves can remain the same. The five elements are: the body, feelings, perceptions, other mental activities, and consciousness. They are always changing. It is true that throughout your life you bear the same name—David or Angelina—but you are changing all the time. It is only your name that does not change. However, the understanding of the name can change. When a person becomes more lovely, his name sounds more lovely too.

Impermanence is the reality of things in the phenomenal world. This is the insight from both East and West. "No one can bathe twice in the same river" is a Western insight. While standing on a bridge, Confucius once said, "Flowing always like this day and night." It is the same kind of insight. If everything is impermanent, there cannot be a permanent entity. This is the meaning of non-self. Non-self does not mean non-person or non-existing. Even though you are non-self, you continue to be a person with a body, with feelings, with perceptions, with mental formations, with consciousness. You continue to be a person, but a person without a separate self.

Is there anything that has a separate self? No. A tree that stands in the front yard does not have a separate self. Without the sunshine, without the clouds, without the air, without the minerals, a tree cannot be there. A tree is made of non-tree elements. Because a tree has no separate existence, we say a tree has no self. The self of the tree is made of the self of the non-tree elements.

Let us not be caught by words. Let us touch reality deeply and transcend all the words. The person is only possible because she is non-self. Because of impermanence and non-self, everything is possible, including the person.

A gentleman in England while studying Buddhism kept repeating that everything is impermanent. He would always complain to his daughter about the impermanence of things. One day his daughter said, "Daddy, if things are not impermanent, how can I grow up?" This is a very intelligent statement. In order for the daughter to grow up, things have to be impermanent, otherwise she would be twelve years old forever. So impermanence is the basic condition for life. Thanks to impermanence, everything is possible.

Democracy is not possible without impermanence. You have the hope of transforming a regime that's not democratic into a democratic one, thanks to impermanence. When you plant a grain of corn into the damp soil, you hope that it will grow to become a corn plant. If things are not impermanent, how can the grain of corn become a plant of corn? If the plant did not mature, produce a seed, and die, how could new corn be possible? This is also from the Bible. Therefore, impermanence and non-self make everything, including the person, possible.

GETTING CAUGHT IN
NOTIONS OF NON-SELF

There are Buddhists who are caught in the notion of non-self. This is a shame, because the Buddha taught impermanence and non-self to help us overcome all notions, including the notion of a separate self. But it does not help if you are caught in the notion of non-self.

There are always some people who are ready to embrace a doctrine, a notion, a dogma, and they miss the real teaching. A monk sitting under a tree was asked by a lady passing by, "Venerable, did you see a lady pass here?" He said, "No, I did not see a lady go by. I only saw a combination of bones and flesh, and the five elements."

This is ridiculous. This monk was caught in the notion of non-self. You can imagine how disappointed the Buddha is when he has a student like that, a student who is caught in the Buddha's teaching of impermanence and non-self. The teaching of impermanence and non-self only aims to show us that everything is connected to everything else, the teaching of interbeing. Without this, the other cannot be. One wave is made of all the other waves. One electron is made of all the other electrons. Nuclear physicists of our time are beginning to speak in this language.

In India, during the sixth century, so many monks and laypeople were caught in the idea of non-self that there was a strong reaction on the part of those who understood Buddhism better. They created a school of Buddhism that taught that there was a self. In the beginning, it looked like they were teaching just the opposite of what the Buddha said, but in fact they were more intelligent than the others. Other people called them personalists, *Pudgalavada* in Sanskrit. *Pudgala* means "the person."

When the famous Xuan Zhuang of China came to India to learn Buddhism, there were more than sixty thousand monks who belonged to the school of Pudgalavada. Many of them liked the idea that "the person is." I think that those monks could speak to our Protestant and Catholic brothers and sisters very well because they realized that even when you accept the teaching and the practice of non-self and impermanence, you still are a person.

One of the sentences that the *Pudgalavada* monks quoted in the Sutra was, "There is a person whose appearance in the world is for the benefit of many. Who is that person? The *Tathagatha* (The Buddha)." They mean in Buddhist scriptures there are sentences that include the word "person," even to denote the person of the Buddha.

"HAPPY CONTINUATION DAY!"

Rebirth happens to us daily. Isn't it true that you are reborn in every moment of your daily life? Is it possible for you to renew yourself in every moment of your daily life? Is it possible for you to transform your suffering and your lack of understanding and become a new person?

If you practice looking deeply, you will see that the notion of birth and death can be transcended.

To be born means that from no one you suddenly become someone, from nothing you suddenly become something. That is our idea of birth. But when you look deeply at a wave, you see that a wave does not come from nothing. Nothing can come from nothing. Before a tree is here, it was somewhere else. It was a seed, and before that it was part of another tree. Before the rain is here, it was a cloud. The rain was not born, it is only a transformation of the cloud. It is a continuation. If you look deeply into the rain, you recognize the cloud which is the former life of the rain.

There is no birth, according to the Buddhist teaching. There is only a continuation.

On your birthday, it is advisable that you don't sing, "Happy Birthday," but that instead you sing, "Happy Continuation Day." You have been here, you don't know since when. You have never been born and you are not going to die, because to die means from someone you suddenly become no one. From something, you suddenly become nothing. Nothing is like that. Even when you burn a piece of cloth, it will not become nothing. It will become the heat that penetrates into the cosmos. It will become smoke that rises into the sky to become part of a cloud. It will become some ash that falls to the ground that may manifest tomorrow as a leaf, a blade of grass, or a flower. So there is only a continuation.

Looking deeply helps us transcend the notion of birth and death. *Rebirth* is not such a good word. A better word is *continuation*. Everyone can witness the nature of no birth and no death of all things. Scientists agree that there is no birth and no death of anything. The French scientist Lavoisier said, "Nothing is created and nothing dies" *(Rien ne se crée, rien ne se perd)*. He used the exact words that are used in the *Prajnaparamita Heart Sutra.* I don't think Lavoisier ever practiced the *Heart Sutra.*

If you touch the phenomenal realm deeply, you touch the ultimate realm which is the realm of no birth and no death. The ultimate is nirvana, it is God, and it is available to us twenty-four hours a day.

A Zen teacher in Vietnam of the tenth century, Master Thien Hoi, was asked by a student where to find the world of no birth and no death. The Zen teacher replied, "You find it right in the world of birth and death." It's so simple and so clear. Looking deeply into the nature of something, like a tree, a piece of cloth, or a cloud, you discover the nature of no birth and no death in it. It is very important to have enough time and enough of the energy of mindfulness in us to touch things deeply enough to discover their birthless and deathless nature.

TO BE, OR NOT TO BE

All things have the nature of no coming and no going. The Buddha said that when conditions are sufficient, things reveal themselves. They don't come from anywhere. When conditions are no longer sufficient, things hide themselves. They just do not manifest themselves and become an object of our perception. They don't go anywhere. It is a matter of conditions only.

If we look deeply into the nature of reality, we transcend the notion of coming and going, of being and non-being. When conditions are sufficient, things can be seen by you, and you say that "you are." When conditions are no longer sufficient and things can no longer be seen by you, you use the term "non-being." You say, "You are not." In fact, reality cannot be described in terms of being and non-being. Being and non-being are notions created by you, exactly like the notions of birth and death, and coming and going. So if your beloved one can no longer be seen, it does not mean that from being she has become non-being. If you witness that truth, you will suffer much less. If you witness that truth concerning yourself, you will transcend your fear of dying, of becoming nothing.

Is it true that Buddhism teaches that the reality of everything is non-being? No. Emptiness means the emptiness of a separate existence, the emptiness of a permanent entity, emptiness of all concepts. The teaching of emptiness helps you to transcend the notion of birth and death, the notion of coming and going, and the notion of being and non-being. If you are caught in the notion of being or in the notion of non-being, you cannot touch the ultimate. If you are caught in these concepts, you are not capable of touching the ultimate dimension.

It is therefore not correct to say that Christianity teaches being while Buddhism teaches non-being. If you spend a little time studying Buddhism, you will see that the practice is to transcend both notions of being and non-being. To the Buddhist, "To be or not to be" is not the question. The question is whether or not you can transcend these notions.

TOUCHING THE GROUND OF BEING

In Christianity and Buddhism, in both East and West, we have the notion of "the All," the ultimate reality, the ground of being. Our Christian friends tend to think that Buddhists don't like to conceive of "the All," or the ground of being, as a person. That is what they resist the most. Some Christians believe that to Buddhists, "the All," or the ground of being, is a non-person. But this is not true at all. Perhaps you have already realized this insight in your daily life. Every time you contemplate a tree, although you know that the tree is not a person, your relationship with the tree is not a relationship between a person and a non-person.

THERE IS THINKING
IN THE BLUE SKY

~

When I touch a rock, I never touch it as inanimate. The tree is spirit, mind; the rock is spirit, mind; the air, the stars, the moon, everything is consciousness. They are the object of your consciousness. When you say, "The wind blows," what are you trying to say? You have a perception that the wind is blowing, so you say, "I know the wind is blowing." This is a perception. The wind may be blowing, but the person next to you may not notice it. Because you have the perception that the wind is blowing, you try to tell her the wind is blowing.

To say, "The wind is blowing," is very funny. The wind must be blowing, otherwise it is not the wind. So you don't have to say the word "blowing." You can just say "wind." What is wind? Wind is your perception, your consciousness. According to your perception, the wind is. The only thing you are sure of is that the wind is the object of your perception. Your perception consists of the subject and the object, the perceiver and the perceived. The wind is part of your consciousness. The wind is the object of your perception.

Sometimes you create the object of your perception without any basis. You imagine that another person is trying to destroy you, when in fact she doesn't have that idea at all.

The mind creates many things. In the teaching of the *Dharmalakshana* school, you learn to look at things as objects of your consciousness and not as separate, independent entities. When you look at the sky, if you look deeply you don't see the blue sky as something separate from you, as something inanimate. You perceive the sky as your consciousness. It is the collective consciousness as well. There is a school of thought in Princeton which states that there is *thinking* in the blue sky. There is *thinking* in the cloud, there is *thinking* in the stars. You see sky as consciousness. The sky *is* consciousness, the clouds *are* consciousness, stars *are* consciousness. They are not inanimate objects separated from your consciousness. It is the object of your consciousness so you train like that in order not to see objects of perception as something independent from perceptions. The great consciousness is manifesting itself. Everything is seen as consciousness. In the non-Buddhist spheres, very often they come to the same insight as the Buddha did.

In my experience, when I touch a tree, when I look at a bird, when I contemplate the water in the creek, I admire them not because they have been created by God and not because they have the Buddha nature. I admire them because they are trees, they are rocks, they are water. I bow to a rock because it is a rock. I don't bow to a rock because there is a spirit inhabiting the rock. I also don't consider the rock as an inanimate thing. Because the rock, to me, is nothing less than consciousness, than the spirit itself.

Many of our Christian friends are not happy when Buddhists call that spirit by other names, and don't use the word *God*. Teilhard de Chardin was shocked to hear people calling the Holy Spirit "the All," or "spirit," and not God. But is it safe to use the word *God* when many people think of God as a person in the phenomenal sense? If people know that God is not a person, but is not less than a person, as Paul Tillich said, then it will not be at all difficult to use the word *God*.

The Buddha has so many bodies. He has a physical body, and he has his Dharma body. Before passing away, he told his disciples: "This physical body of mine is not so important. Touch my Dharma body. My Dharma body will be with you."

What is the Dharma? The Dharma is not a set of laws and practices, or a stack of sutras, or videotapes, or cassettes. The Dharma is understanding, it is the practice of loving-kindness as expressed by life. You cannot see the Dharma unless you see a person practicing the Dharma, making the Dharma apparent to everyone, like a nun walking mindfully, touching the Earth deeply, and radiating peace and joy. This nun is not preaching or showing a videotape, but she is expressing the living Dharma. She can express the living Dharma because she is a person. In our physical body we can touch the Dharma body. So the Buddha has a Dharma body, and his Dharma body will continue to be seen and touched by us as long as there are people who continue to practice the Dharma. All of this is possible only with non-self, with impermanence.

LOVING BUDDHA, LOVING GOD

When we speak of loving the Buddha, what do we mean? Do we need to love the Buddha? Does the

Buddha need to be loved by us? We practice invoking the name of the Buddha, and the recollection of the Buddha, to make the Buddha present in our mind, to bring him into our moments in daily life. Does the Buddha need us to love him, to remember him, to glorify him? I don't think so. I don't think that the Buddha needs love. We may feel love for the Buddha, the way we feel love for our parents and our teachers. The Buddha is our teacher. Of course we have admiration for our teacher, the Buddha. The Buddha has practiced well, he has courage. He has a lot of compassion, and understanding, and he is a free person. He does not suffer a lot like us because he has a great deal of understanding, compassion, and loving-kindness. You love someone when that someone needs you. When that someone suffers, your love relieves his or her suffering. Your love is to bring happiness to him or to her. That is the meaning of love. It is easy to understand that living beings around you who suffer need your love. But does your salvation, your liberation, depend on your loving the Buddha? I don't think so. If you praise the Buddha, it is not because the Buddha wants you to praise him or her.

Yet while praising the Buddha, you are touching and watering the wholesome seeds in you. According to this practice, the Buddha is mindfulness, under-standing, and love. When you touch the seed of un-derstanding, mindfulness, and loving-kindness in you, you make these qualities grow stronger for your own happiness, and for the happiness of other peo-ple and living beings around you. When you burn in-cense, it is not for the Buddha. The Buddha does not need your incense. But when you burn the in-cense, make deep bows, and praise the Buddha, you water the wholesome seeds in you. This is the prac-tice. When you become mindful, understanding, and loving, you suffer much less, you begin to feel happy, and the people around you begin to profit from your being there.

When a Christian says that she does things in a particular way because she loves God, what does she mean? How does she love God? Does she love God in the same way that she loves her father, her mother, or her teacher? Her father, mother, or teacher may have difficulties. They may suffer and need her love and support. I don't think God needs this kind of love and support. In Christianity, when you love God you have to love your neighbor, otherwise you can-not say that you love God. Then you have to go fur-ther. You have to love your enemy.

THE BIRTH OF
UNDERSTANDING

~

Why do you have to love your enemy? How can you love your enemy?

In the Buddhist teaching, this is very clear. Buddhism teaches that understanding is the ground of love. When you are mindful, you realize that the other person suffers. You see her suffering and suddenly you don't want her to suffer any more. You know that there are things you can refrain from doing to make her stop suffering, and there are things you can do to bring her relief.

When you begin to see the suffering in the other person, compassion is born, and you no longer consider that person as your enemy. You can love your enemy. The moment you realize that your so-called enemy suffers and you want him to stop suffering, he ceases to be your enemy.

When we hate someone, we are angry at him because we do not understand him or his environment. By practicing deep looking, we realize that if we grew up like him, in his set of circumstances and having lived in his environment, we would be just like him.

That kind of understanding removes your anger, removes your discrimination, and suddenly that person is no longer your enemy. Then you can love him. As long as he or she remains an enemy, love is impossible. Loving your enemy is only possible when you don't see him as your enemy any more, and the only way to do this is by practicing deep looking. That person has made you suffer quite a lot in the past. The practice is to ask why.

When you are unhappy, your unhappiness spills all around you. If you have learned the art of understanding and tolerance, then you will suffer much less. Looking at living beings with compassionate eyes makes you feel wonderful. You do not change anything. You only practice seeing with the eyes of compassion, and suddenly you suffer much less. What are the eyes of compassion? The eyes are to look and to understand. The heart is to love. "The eyes of compassion" means the eyes that look and understand. If there is understanding, compassion will arise in a very natural way. "The eyes of compassion" means the eyes of deep looking, the eyes of understanding.

THE BIRTH OF LOVE

In Buddhism we learn that understanding is the very foundation of love. If understanding is not there, no matter how hard you try, you cannot love. If you say, "I have to try to love him," this is nonsense. You have to understand him and by doing so you will love him. One of the things I have learned from the teaching of the Buddha is that without understanding, love is not possible. If a husband and wife do not understand each other, they cannot love each other. If a father and son do not understand each other, they will make each other suffer. So understanding is the key that unlocks the door to love.

Understanding is the process of looking deeply. Meditation means to look deeply at things, to touch things deeply. A wave has to realize that there are other waves around her. Each wave has her own suffering. You are not the only person who suffers. Your sisters and your brothers also suffer. The moment you see the suffering in them, you stop blaming them, and you stop the suffering in you. If you suffer and if you believe that your suffering is created by the people around you, you have to look again. Most of your suffering comes from the lack of understanding of yourself and others.

In Buddhism, I don't think that compassion and loving-kindness are practiced for the sake of our individual salvation. The truth taught by the Buddha is that suffering exists. If you touch suffering deeply in yourself and in the other person, understanding will arise. When understanding arises, love and acceptance will also arise, and they will bring the suffering to an end.

You may believe that your suffering is greater than anyone else's, or that you are the only person who suffers. But this is not true. When you recognize the suffering around you it will help you to suffer less. Get out of yourself and look. Christmas is an opportunity for us to do this. Suffering is in me, of course, but it is also in you. Suffering is in the world.

There was a person who was born nearly two thousand years ago. He was aware that suffering was going on in him and in his society, and he did not hide himself from the suffering. Instead, he came out to investigate deeply the nature of suffering, the causes of suffering. Because he had the courage to speak out, he became the teacher of many generations. The best way to celebrate Christmas may be to practice mindful walking, mindful sitting, and looking deeply into things, to discover that suffering is still there in every one of us and in the world. Just by recognizing suffering we relieve our hearts of the suffering that has been weighing on us for so many days and months. According to the Buddhist teaching, when you touch suffering deeply, you will understand the nature of suffering and then the way to happiness will reveal itself.

In Buddhism, nirvana is described as peace, stability, and freedom. The practice is to realize that peace, stability, and freedom are available to us right here and now, twenty-four hours a day. We only need to know how to touch them, and we have to have the intention, the determination, to do so. It's like the water that is always available to the wave. It is only a matter of the wave touching the water and realizing that it is there.

TWO

GOING HOME

Dear friends, today is the twenty-eighth of December 1995, and we are in the Upper Hamlet.

Christmas and New Year's are opportunities for us to go home. In Asia, the Lunar New Year is considered a time for people to go back to their home, their roots. If you are Chinese or Vietnamese, you go back to your family home that day. This is an opportunity for people to see each other again after some time of being apart from each other. During the time they are together, they practice connecting with each other and with their ancestors. To practice going home, to practice getting in touch with our ancestors, is what everyone wants to do on New Year's Day.

OUR TRUE HOME

When you practice the bell of mindfulness, you breathe in, and you listen deeply to the sound of the bell, and you say, "Listen, listen." Then you breathe out and you say, "This wonderful sound brings me back to my true home." Our true home is something we all want to go back to. Some of us feel we don't have a home.

What is the meaning of "true home"? In the last Dharma talk, we talked about a wave. Does a wave have a home? When a wave looks deeply into herself, she will realize the presence of all the other waves. When we are mindful, fully living each moment of our daily lives, we may realize that everyone and everything around us is our home. Isn't it true that the air we breathe is our home, that the blue sky, the rivers, the mountains, the people around us, the trees, and the animals are our home? A wave looking deeply into herself will see that she is made up of all the other waves and will no longer feel she is cut off from everything around her. She will be able to recognize that the other waves are also her home. When you practice walking meditation, walk in such a way that you recognize your home, in the here and the now. See the trees as your home, the air as your home, the blue sky as your home, and the earth that you tread as your home. This can only be done in the here and the now.

Sometimes we have a feeling of alienation. We feel lonely and as if we are cut off from everything. We have been a wanderer and have tried hard but have never been able to reach our true home. However, we all have a home, and this is our practice, the practice of going home.

It's funny. In my country, the husband refers to his wife as "my home." The wife refers to her husband as "my home." Talking with another person she might say, "My home said that" or "My home is not here at the moment." There must be some feeling behind this.

When we say, "Home sweet home," where is it? When we practice looking deeply, we realize that our home is everywhere. We have to be able to see that the trees are our home and the blue sky is our home. It looks like a difficult practice, but it's really easy. You only need to stop being a wanderer in order to be at home. "Listen, listen. This wonderful sound brings me back to my true home." The voice of the Buddha, the sound of the bell, the sunshine, everything is calling us back to our true home. Once you are back in your true home, you'll feel the peace and the joy you deserve.

If you are a Christian, you feel that Jesus Christ is your home. It's very comfortable to think of Jesus as your home. If you are a Buddhist, then it's very nice to think of the Buddha as your home. Your home is available in the here and the now. Christ is there, the Buddha is there. The practice is how to touch them, how to touch your home. You call Christ "the Living Christ," so you cannot believe that Christ is only someone who lived in the past, and is no longer there. He is ever-present. Your practice is how to touch him; he is your home. If you are a Buddhist, you practice very much in the same way. You invoke the name of the Buddha as one of the ways to touch the Buddha, because you know that he is your home. The living Christ, the living Buddha is your home.

But the living Christ is not only a notion, or an idea. He must be a reality. This is true for the living Buddha, too. How can you recognize the presence of the living Christ or the living Buddha? This is your practice. Maybe when you hear the sound of the bell, you are able to recognize him, to touch your true home. Maybe because you know how to walk mindfully, with concentration, you recognize your home.

What is the home of a wave? The home of the wave is all the other waves, and the home of the wave is water. If the wave is capable of touching himself and the other waves very deeply, he will realize that he is made of water. Being aware that he is water, he transcends all discrimination, sorrows, and fears. Your home is available in the here and the now. Your home is Jesus or God. Your home is Buddha, or Buddhahood.

A PERSON?
OR MORE THAN A PERSON?

Last week we spoke of nirvana as the reality of no birth and no death.

Nirvana is our true substance just as water is the true substance of the wave. We practice to realize that nirvana is our substance. Once we realize this, we transcend the fear of birth and death, of being and non-being. God is an equivalent expression. God is the foundation of being, or as many theologians, like Paul Tillich, say, "God is the ground of being."

Last week we said that the notion of being and

non-being cannot be applied to God or to nirvana. The notion of beginning and end cannot be applied to the absolute either. That is why both the notion of person and of non-person cannot be applied to God nor can it be applied to nirvana. So if we spend time quarreling with each other as to whether God is a person or a non-person, we waste our time. That is discouraged in the Buddhist practice and that is why Paul Tillich was so skillful when he said, "God is not a person, but not less than a person." It was a wonderful way to advise people not to spend too much time speculating.

We are people, but we are also more than just people. Are you only a person? Or at the same time are you also a tree and a rock? You only need to look deeply to discover that you are a person and at the same time you are a rock and a tree. In the Buddhist circle, people believe that in former lives they were human beings, animals, plants, and minerals. This is scientifically true. If we look deeply into the evolution of our species, we see that in former times we have been a rock, a tree, and an animal. Humans are very young creatures. We have evolved over many years to become what we are today. It is scientifically proven that we have been a rock, a cloud, a tree, a rabbit, a deer, a rose, and a single-cell being.

If you continue to look deeply, you will see that in the present moment, you continue to be a rose, a rabbit, a tree, and a rock. This is the truth of interbeing. You are made of non-you elements. You can touch the cloud within you. You can touch the sunshine within you. You can touch the trees and the earth within you. You know that if these elements were not in you, you could not be here at this very moment. Not only in former lives were you a tree, but sitting here, right now, you are a tree. That is why I say that the trees are your home. Recognize your home, your home sweet home.

CULTIVATING OUR HOME, CULTIVATING THE HOLY

In East Asia, we speak of the human body as a mini-cosmos. The cosmos is our home, and we can touch it by being aware of our body. Meditation is to be still: to sit still, to stand still, and to walk with stillness. Meditation means to look deeply, to touch deeply so we can realize we are already home. Our home is available right here and now.

Jesus Christ practiced meditation. When John

baptized Jesus, he made it possible for the Holy Spirit to be born, or manifested, in Jesus the human being. Then Jesus went to the mountain to spend forty days in retreat. He practiced meditation and strengthened that Spirit in order to bring about a total transformation. Although it's not recorded in what position he practiced, I am sure he did sitting and walking meditation, and that he practiced looking deeply, touching deeply, and nourishing the energy of the Holy Spirit in him. Maybe he sat under a Bodhi tree like the Buddha.

Jesus had the power to bring joy, happiness, and healing to others because the energy of the Holy Spirit was full inside him. We have the seed of the Holy Spirit in us. In the Buddhist circle we speak of Buddhahood. We speak of mindfulness. Mindfulness is the energy that helps us be still; to be present to look deeply and touch deeply so that we begin to understand and realize that we are home.

The image of Jesus that is presented to us is usually of Jesus on the cross. This is a very painful image for me. It does not convey joy or peace, and this does not do justice to Jesus. I hope that our Christian friends will also portray Jesus in other ways, like sitting in the lotus position or doing walking meditation. Doing so will allow us to feel peace and joy penetrating into our hearts when we contemplate Jesus. This is my suggestion.

FINDING REFUGE
IN THE ISLAND OF SELF

In the Buddhist tradition, we practice taking refuge instead of receiving baptism. With a teacher and Sangha, or spiritual community, surrounding you, you join your palms, and say, "I take refuge in the Buddha. I take refuge in the Dharma. I take refuge in the Sangha." That also is the practice of going home. Your home is the Buddha, the Dharma, and the Sangha, and they are all available in the present moment. You don't have to go to India to practice the Three Refuges. You can be right here to practice taking refuge. Your practice will determine if the feeling of being at home in yourself is deep or not.

When the Buddha was eighty years old and was about to die, he told his disciples they should take refuge in the island of self *(attadipa)*. Because if they go back to themselves and look deeply, they will touch the Buddha, the Dharma, and the Sangha in themselves. This still remains a very important practice for all of us. Every time you feel lost, alienated, cut off from life, or from the world, every time you feel despair, anger, or instability, you have to know how to practice going home. Mindful breathing is the vehicle that you use to go back to your true home where you meet the Buddha, the Dharma, and the Sangha. Mindful breathing brings you home—it generates the energy of mindfulness in you. Mindfulness is the substance of a Buddha.

The Sangha, the community, is a wonderful home. Every time you go back to the Sangha, you feel that you can breathe easier, you can walk more mindfully, and you can more fully enjoy the blue sky, the white clouds, and the cypress tree in your yard. Why? Because the Sangha members practice going home all day, through walking, breathing, cooking, and doing their daily activities mindfully.

It's strange. You have been to Plum Village and received instructions on how to breathe, walk, smile, and take refuge; you took these back to your home and practiced. Yet whenever you return to Plum Village, you find that with the Sangha you can practice better than when you were home alone. There are things that you don't do easily when you are alone. But surrounded by members of the Sangha, suddenly these things become easy. You don't need to make much effort to do them, and you enjoy doing them a lot. If you had an experience like this, try to build a Sangha where you live. A Sangha is our refuge. Taking refuge in the Sangha is not a matter of faith, or belief; it is a matter of practice. Talk to your child, your companion, and your friends about the necessity of having a Sangha. If you have a Sangha, you are safe. You can nourish your home and protect yourself. You can enlarge your home all the time to include the clouds, the trees, and the walking meditation path. As you have learned, everything belongs to our home, everything belongs to our Sangha.

You may think that if a person does not believe in the practice, he or she cannot be part of your Sangha. But if he or she is surrounded by three, four, or five people who practice mindful breathing, mindful walking, mindful sitting, and smiling, one day that person may realize that she is more than herself. Even if you don't talk to him or her about your practice, she will realize that there is something in you that keeps you fresh, calm, and happy. You have the Sangha, the Dharma, and the Buddha in you. After that you'll be able to invite him or her into your Sangha. Taking refuge in the Sangha is very important. Not a day goes by when I do not practice taking refuge several times.

DARLING, YOU ARE MY HOME

I practice going home by walking, sitting, and doing things in mindfulness so I do not lose myself. Tinh Thuy, a permanent resident at Plum Village, wrote a song several years ago entitled "I Am Always with Me." The first lines are: "I have been living in myself for a long time. I have never lost myself. I have always been with myself. I have never lost myself."

This is a very important practice. Live your daily life in a way that you never lose yourself. When you are carried away with your worries, fears, cravings, anger, and desire, you run away from yourself and you lose yourself. The practice is always to go back to oneself. You have a wonderful vehicle. And you don't have to buy any gasoline. Mindful breathing and mindful walking are wonderful ways to go back to oneself.

When I meet myself, I see a lot of space. When you are there with yourself, taking care of yourself, there is space in you, vast enough for the white clouds to travel in.

Tinh Thuy's song continues: "I still have my future. I still have my past. That is why I feel light and happy today." Where is your future? Where is your past? You can discover your future, and your past, just by going back to yourself. Of course your ancestors are there within you. When you go back to yourself, you touch your ancestors. Your grandpa and grandma, your father and mother are alive in you. Your ancestors have never died. They are still in you. You only need to practice mindful breathing to touch them and smile at them.

In former lives you were a tree, a rock, a cloud, a rabbit, a deer. All these things are still in you and you can touch them. They belong to your home. Go back and touch these elements and you will see that your Dharma body is huge and your home is vast. Your brothers and sisters, your children and their children, your students and their students are there. They are not just around you; they are within you.

Imagine a lemon tree in springtime. There are a lot of beautiful white lemon blossoms. You don't see any lemons on the tree, yet you know that the lemons are already there. Because the lemon blossoms are there, the lemons are there. So even if you are still young, you can touch your children and your grandchildren within you. Your children and your grandchildren also constitute your home.

You have to be able to look at the cypress tree, breathing in, breathing out, smiling, and tell the cypress, "Darling, you are my home." Touch deeply the earth that you tread: "Darling, you are my home."

The Earth can be a mother, she can be a sister. Why do you have to run to find your home? Your home is here, your home is now. Recognize it. Everything, everyone is part of your true home. You have a lot of space. You are not isolated. You are us and you can embrace us as your home. *Us* means a cypress tree, a deer, a rabbit, and so on.

Every one of us needs a home. The world needs a home. There are so many young people who are homeless. They may have a building to live in, but they are homeless in their hearts. That is why the most important practice of our time is to give each person a home. Be a home for them. Each of us has to serve as the home for others. When we look at something or someone, be it a person, a tree, or anything, look at it in such a way that we touch them as part of our home. "Here is the Pure Land, the Pure Land is here." That is the beginning of a song we like to sing in Plum Village. The Pure Land is our true home.

AT HOME IN
THE DHARMA BODY

It is very fortunate that you have Jesus Christ as your home. He is a reality. One of the conditions that helps you to recognize and identify him as your home is that he was a human being. What if we only have an idea, a notion of God? God is concrete in the form of a human being: God the Son, Jesus Christ.

It is also fortunate that in Buddhism, the *Dharmakaya*, the body of the Dharma, is embodied in a very concrete way, by the presence of a human being, the Buddha Shakyamuni. It's much easier for you to touch the absolute, the ultimate, when you are able to touch a human being. That is why we tend to think of God as a human being, as having a body. God as a person.

Buddhists sometimes visualize the Dharmakaya, the body of the absolute, in the form of a human being too. There is Shakyamuni, a human being, who embodies the Dharma. Buddhism teaches that you have many bodies including a physical body and a Dharma body. You carry within you the body of the Dharma, and it is possible for you to touch it. You also have the Buddha body that you can touch at any time.

The expression *Dharma body* was already being used during the time of the Buddha. When the monk Vaikhali was sick, the Buddha went to visit him at the house of a potter. Vaikhali loved and admired the Buddha very much. In the beginning of his practice as a monk, he spent hours and hours sitting near the Buddha, just contemplating the physical body of the Buddha. Gradually Vaikhali tried to go beyond the physical body of the Buddha and touch the Dharma body of the Buddha. He was dying, and the Buddha asked, "Vaikhali, how do you feel in your body?" Vaikhali said, "Lord, I suffer so much. The pain in my body is increasing." The Buddha said, "Vaikhali, do you have peace in yourself? Do you have any regrets?" Vaikhali said, "No, Lord. I don't have any regrets concerning my practice. I have peace in me. But there is only a little regret in me that because I am sick, I can no longer visit you on the Gridhakuta Mountain any more." The Buddha said, "Come on, Vaikhali, this physical body is not the most important thing. If you have touched the Dharma, if you live every minute with the Dharma, then my Dharma body is always with you."

The Dharma body is the body of the teaching. You can discover your Dharma body by yourself. A teacher, brother, or sister can also help you discover your Dharma body. Your practice is a process of discovering your Dharma body. The deeper you touch the Dharma body, the happier you are, and the greater your peace will be.

The Dharma body isn't given to you by someone else. It is deep within you and it is a matter of discovering it. When you practice walking meditation, you can release your anger and sorrow. You can look more deeply into the reality of things and get rid of all your illusions, cravings, and desires. That means that you have the body of the Dharma within you. You will suffer less if you know how to make use of your Dharma body. You'll be freer, more peaceful, and happier. The Buddha and the Sangha can help you touch deeply the Dharma body within you. Since the Dharma body is deep in you, the Buddha body is also there. You are a Buddha-to-be. You carry with you your physical body, your Dharma body, and your Buddha body.

BEYOND THE BODY OF GOD

Scientists like to speak in the language of mathematics. There are many good mathematicians among us. Those of us who look at reality and speak about reality in the language of mathematics find that there is no other language that can speak as well as mathematics does about reality. When a mathematician admires reality in terms of mathematics, he has the tendency to believe that God is the best mathematician. Otherwise how could things be arranged in such a way? If God is not a mathematician, how could he create things perfectly in this way?

The artist, the painter, who uses colors and brushes

to create beautiful images on canvas, tends to believe that God is the best of all painters. Look around you. Nothing is more beautiful than what you see—the morning sunrise, the splendid sunset, the ocean, the stars, the leaves, the trees, the clouds—everything is so beautiful. If God is not the best of all painters, how could he have created the world as it is? Painters have the right to think of God as the best painter.

Let us look at the fish swimming very happily in the water. He tends to think of God as the best of swimmers. It is very normal for human beings to conceive of God as a human being. It is said that God has created man in his own image. But it may be true that humankind has created God in the image of humankind. Both statements are true. To spend our time quarreling with each other as to whether God is a person or not is just a waste of our time. You are a person, but you are more than a person. This can be applied to the cosmos, to the spirit, and to God.

THE BODY OF FAITH

In Buddhism, people consider faith as a source of energy. With faith, with the energy of faith, you are more alive. But faith in what? That is the question. When you see or hear something, you may be convinced that that something is true, good, and beautiful. Suddenly you have faith in that something. But be aware that the object of your faith may not be there for a long time. You may lose your faith a few hours later, or a few days later because what you saw or heard was not a right perception. When you put your belief into practice, you find it does not work. So you lose your faith. When you put your belief into practice, you may find that it works, but later on, when you try to do the same thing again, it does not work and you lose your faith again. Why? The answer is that faith is a living thing. Faith has to grow. If your faith is just a notion, it is not a living thing. When you conceive of an idea and cling to it as the object of your faith, you risk losing your faith later on.

Faith has to do with understanding and knowing. Suppose you see someone make tofu. You believe that you did not miss any details so you have faith that you can make tofu by yourself. You go and get all the ingredients together and attempt to make tofu, but it does not work. You are unable to make tofu. So you go back to the other person and ask her to teach you again. Now you make the tofu in her presence to make sure that you do it correctly. After making it successfully, you have faith that you can make tofu. You tell yourself no one can remove your faith in your ability to make tofu. You may believe that your way of making tofu is the only way, or the best way. But one or two years later, you may meet a person who makes tofu in a very different way, and his tofu tastes better. You learn more, and you improve your art of making tofu. Your faith in making tofu is a living thing. It depends on your depth of seeing and understanding.

In the Buddhist circle, people speak about letting go of your knowledge. When you know something, you stick to your knowledge. You are not ready to let it go, and this is an obstacle on the path of practice. In Buddhism, knowledge can be seen as an obstacle. Many people try to accumulate knowledge, and one day they may realize that the knowledge they possess has become an obstacle to their understanding. The Sanskrit word for "knowledge as obstacle" is *jneyavarana.*

To know and to understand are two different things. When you climb a ladder, unless you abandon the lower step, you will not be able to climb to a higher one. Knowledge is like that. If you are not ready to let go of your knowledge, you cannot get a deeper knowledge of the same thing. The history of science proves this. You discover a new thing that helps you to understand better. Yet you are aware that some day you'll have to let go of that thing in order to discover something deeper and higher. The Buddhist teaching of abandoning your knowledge is very important.

The process of learning and understanding has to do with your faith. As you let go of one notion, one understanding, your faith grows. The kind of Buddhism that you learned when you were twenty years old, you have let go of. The notion of Buddha you had when you were fifteen is quite different from your understanding of the Buddha now. Your understanding of the Buddha is deeper and closer to reality now. But you know that you have to let your notions go in order to have a deeper understanding of the Buddha.

Your faith is also changing as a function of your understanding. Faith is a living thing, and its food is understanding. This is very important and we have to remember this. If we cling to a notion or if we believe that that notion is the highest truth, we'll get lost. If you believe that your knowledge is the highest peak of human knowledge, you'll get lost. That kind of belief is not considered right belief.

So you have to be ready to let go of your notion of God, your understanding of Jesus, your notion of Buddha, and your understanding of the Buddha. You know that when climbing a ladder, you have to abandon the lower step in order to come to a higher one. Although you abandon it, you know the lower step has served you. It has been useful in the process of your learning and practice.

Because you have to grow in your spiritual life, you cannot just stick to an idea. Suppose you are in danger or trouble, and you don't know what to do. You kneel down and pray to God, or to Avalokitesvara, the Bodhisattva of Compassionate Listening. Suddenly things turn out fine and you believe in the power of prayer. It may happen that the next time you get into the same kind of trouble and you kneel down and pray, it doesn't work. Then you might lose your faith in God, or in the Bodhisattva Avalokitesvara. This is an occasion for you to examine your understanding, and your way of praying. To lose your faith is something unpleasant and you can suffer a great deal. The Buddha warned us several times that we have to be careful about our knowledge.

FAITH IS A LIVING THING

The word *siksa*, or learning, in Buddhism does not mean you learn with your intellect. You learn with your body also. You have to train to practice, for example, mindful breathing. You have to really practice and you have to train so that you can enjoy every breath you take. And when you have succeeded, you don't need to train anymore. You just live normally and you do it perfectly. We call that stage the stage of no more learning. No learning. It does not mean that person has no education. It does mean that he or she no longer needs education. But education here means practicing. Not with the intellect, but with the whole person.

We like to train in chanting, in walking, and in breathing. In medical school, there's also training. We can train to be a doctor or an architect. We learn with the mind, the body, with everything. Transformation is part of training. Man is an animal, so if animals need to be trained, then man needs to be trained. Animals may be trained against their will. But we want to be trained to be happy.

All of us practice walking meditation. First you receive some instructions from a teacher, or a brother, or a sister, and you use your body and your life to experiment with the practice. Those who have practiced walking meditation for some time have seen changes in their practice. Their way of practicing walking meditation brings more peace, awareness, and joy to them than when they first began practicing. Our understanding of practice grows. Suppose you have faith in walking meditation. That faith in walking meditation is made of your experience of practice. You do better and better all the time because you have practiced and you have learned. You are doing better than the year before, just because in the last year you have practiced continuously. You have found better ways to practice. Now you can release your anger, your worries, and you can restore your peace and your health by practicing walking meditation.

Our faith in the practice also grows. What I am saying is simple: Faith is a living thing. It has to grow. The food that helps it to grow is the continued discoveries, the deeper understanding of reality. In Buddhism, faith is nourished by understanding. The practice of looking deeply helps you to understand better. As you understand better, your faith grows.

As understanding and faith are living things, there is something in our understanding and faith that dies in every moment, and there is something in our understanding and faith that is born every moment. In Zen Buddhism, it is expressed in a very drastic way. Master Lin Chi said, "Be aware. If you meet the Buddha, kill him." I think that's the strongest way of saying this. If you have a notion of the Buddha, you are caught in it. If you don't release the notion of the

Buddha, there is no way for you to advance on the spiritual path. Kill the Buddha. Kill the notion of the Buddha that you have. We have to grow. Otherwise we will die on our spiritual path.

Understanding is a process. It is a living thing. Never claim that you have understood reality completely. As you continue to live deeply each moment of your daily life, your understanding grows as does your faith.

Concentration is the food of understanding. You have to be concentrated for understanding to be possible. When you want to solve a mathematical problem, you have to be concentrated. You cannot turn on the radio and let your mind be dispersed. When you are standing in front of a tree, you have to concentrate on the tree. This brings you understanding of the tree. In our daily life, we have to live in a concentrated way. When eating, you have to eat in concentration. When drinking, you drink in concentration. *Samadhi* is the concentration which makes our mind calm and allows us to look deeply into the object of our concentration. Samadhi practice is very important. You have to dwell in concentration all day. Walking, you dwell firmly in the walking. Sitting, you dwell firmly in the sitting. Breathing, you are fully aware of your breathing.

Concentration also has its food, which is called

mindfulness. Mindfulness is to be here now. Eating mindfully, walking mindfully, sitting mindfully, and hugging mindfully is where you develop concentration. Because you are concentrated, you are able to understand. If you are able to understand, your faith is strengthened. Mindfulness, energy, diligence.

When you have faith, you have a lot of energy in yourself. When you believe in the Buddha, the Dharma, and the Sangha, when you believe in something really good, true, and beautiful, you have a lot of energy in yourself. You are very alive. A person who does not have anything to believe in is without energy. When you have the energy of faith in you, your steps become firmer, your look becomes brighter. You are ready to love, to understand, to help, and to work. If you practice mindfulness well and are devoted to the practice of mindfulness, it is because you have energy in yourself. If you have energy within you, it is because you have faith in the practice, in the Dharma.

Today we speak about faith not as a notion but as something very alive, something that must be nourished by true understanding. In the Buddhist circle, it is repeated again and again that your faith should be right faith. Faith is not made of notions and concepts. Right faith is nourished by your true understanding, not by the intellect but by your experience. It is true faith. I think that in Buddhist-Christian dialogue, faith is a very important topic of inquiry.

THE SANGHA IS
THE DOORWAY

According to what I have said, the Sangha is the door of our true home. Therefore, Sangha-building must be our daily practice. We practice mindfulness in order to realize that everything around us can be an element of our Sangha. Everything around us can be part of our true home.

We know that in every society, every nation, the problem of giving each person a home is important. There are so many homeless people. Spiritually speaking, many of us do not have a home to go back to. That is why the practice of taking refuge is so important. We have to learn to go home every day, and our home is available in the here and in the now. Our living faith is our home.

THREE

LET THE CHILD
BE BORN TO US

Dear friends, it is Christmas Eve 1996. Welcome to the Full Moon Meditation Hall here in the New Hamlet of Plum Village. It is a quarter past three p.m. on the twenty-fourth of December 1996. We are in our Winter Retreat. Welcome to those of you who have just come yesterday or today. Our retreat is a kind of home for you to come back to.

Christmas is often described as a festival for children. I tend to agree with that because who among us is not a child or has not been a child? The child in us is always alive; maybe we have not had enough time to take care of the child within us. To me, it is possible for us to help the child within us to be reborn again and again, because the spirit of the child is the Holy Spirit, it is the spirit of the Buddha. There is no discrimination. A child is always able to live in the present moment. A child can also be free of worries and fear about the future. Therefore, it is very important for us to practice in such a way that the child in us can be reborn.

Let the child be born to us.

Tonight we celebrate the birth of a person who is very dear to humanity, a person who has brought light to the world, Jesus Christ. We hope that children like him will be born to us every moment of our daily lives.

In the Buddhist tradition, we practice Beginning Anew; it is a very important practice. To begin anew means we are reborn fresh and new and able to start again. This is really the good news. The teaching of Buddha offers us ways to be reborn in each moment of our daily life and to learn to love again. There are those who are so discouraged that they no longer have the courage to love. They have suffered a great deal just because they have made an attempt to love and have not succeeded. The wounds within them are so deep that it makes them afraid to try again. We are aware of the presence of these people among us, all around us. We have to bring them the message that love is possible because our world desperately needs love.

In Buddhism, we speak of the mind of love, *bodhicitta*. When you are motivated by the desire to transcend suffering, to get out of a difficult situation and to help others to do the same, you get a powerful source of energy that helps you to do what you want to do to transform yourself and to help other people. That is what we call bodhicitta, the mind of love. It comes from a strong feeling that you don't want to suffer anymore. You want people not to be caught anymore in that kind of situation. This is enlightenment, the kind of enlightenment that gives rise to a powerful source of energy in you called "the mind of love," or "the mind of enlightenment." This is a very important beginning. And if you manage to keep that source of energy alive in you, you can confront any kind of obstacles and you will be able to overcome them. That is why bodhicitta is so important. If we have the energy of love, if we have bodhicitta in us, then we will be filled with life. We will be strong; not afraid of anything because love will help us overcome all difficulties and despair.

True love is made of understanding—understanding the other person, the object of your love, understanding their suffering, their difficulties, and their true aspiration. Out of understanding there will be kindness, there will be compassion, there will be an offering of joy. There will also be a lot of space, because true love is a love without possessiveness. You love and still you are free, and the other person is also free. The kind of love that has no joy is not true love. If both parties cry every day, then that's not true love. There must be joy and freedom and understanding in love.

The next Buddha who will come to us is described as the Buddha of Love, Maitreya. We practice in order to make his or her appearance become a reality. We are preparing the ground for the Buddha-to-come. The next Buddha may be a Sangha, a community of practice, a community of people who share the same values, and not just an individual person, because love is to be practiced collectively. We need each other for the practice to be successful, the practice of love realized by many people at the same time.

Love is a kind of energy. In the Buddhist tradition, we can identify the nature of that energy. We can recognize it when it is there. When love is not true love we are able to know that it is not true love. But when it is true love we are able to recognize it as true love. This is one of our practices.

Love here can also be described as faith, because

faith is a source of energy that can sustain us, that can give us strength. Love and faith are also something to cultivate. They are not just ideas or the commitment to a number of concepts and dogmas. Love is a living thing, faith also. In the process of love, you learn a lot. You love better, you make fewer mistakes. You are more capable of being happy and making other people happy. That develops your faith in your ability to love. So faith is made of very concrete elements—it is made of your true spiritual experience, your experience in your daily life. And faith here is not being caught in an idea or a dogma or a doctrine. Faith is the outcome of your life. It grows. As faith continues to grow, you continue to get the energy because faith is also energy like love. If we look deeply into the nature of our love, we will also see our faith. When we have faith in us, we are no longer afraid of anything.

People who do not believe in anything are those who suffer the most. They don't see anything beautiful, or true, or good. They are in complete confusion. That is the utmost kind of suffering. They might suffer more deeply than any others we might encounter.

When you don't believe in anything, you become sort of a wandering soul; you don't know where to go or what to do. You don't see any meaning in being alive. Because of that, you may try to destroy yourself physically and mentally. And there are so many ways of self-destruction available today.

THE BIRTH OF TRUE FAITH

If there is a distinction between true love and the kind of love that can only engender suffering and despair, the same can be said of faith. There is a kind of faith that sustains us and continues to give us strength and joy. Then there is the kind of faith that may disappear one morning or one evening and leave us completely lonely and lost.

When you have faith, you have the impression that you have the truth, you have insight, you know the path to follow, to take. And that is why you are a happy person. But is it a real path, or just the clinging to a set of beliefs? These are two different things. True faith comes from how the path you are taking can bring you life and love and happiness everyday. You continue to learn so that your happiness and your peace, and the happiness and peace of the people around you, can grow. You don't have to follow a religious path in order to have faith. But if you are committed only to a set of ideas and dogmas that may be called faith, that is not true faith. We have to distinguish. That is not true faith, but it gives you energy. That energy is still blind and can lead to suffering; it can cause suffering for other people around you. Having the kind of energy that can keep you lucid, loving, and tolerant is very different from having energy that is blind. You can make a lot of mistakes out of that kind of energy. We have to distinguish between true faith and blind faith. That is a problem in every tradition.

In the teaching of the Buddha, faith is made of a substance called insight or direct experience. When a teacher knows something, he or she wants to transmit that to disciples. But she cannot transmit the experience, she can only transmit the idea. The disciple has to work through it by himself. The problem is not to communicate the experience in terms of ideas or notions. The issue is how to help the disciple go through the same kind of experience. For instance, you know how a mango tastes, and you may like to try to describe the taste of the mango, but it is better to offer the disciple a piece of mango so that he can have a direct experience. If you write a book on Zen Buddhism, you can do a lot of research. You can read one hundred books, or two hundred books, and you can use that knowledge to write the book on Zen. But that book won't be very helpful because it does not come from your living, from your direct, experience.

Enlightenment, freedom, and transformation happen through direct experience. That is true knowledge, not an intellectual conception of it. Deep understanding of what is there as the object of your perception is true knowledge. Insight is also direct experience. Insight cannot be just a concept that you get while talking to another person. When you talk to another person, maybe that triggers some kind of understanding in you, and that is also direct experience. The insight really comes from you and not from what the other person said.

The confusion, the suffering you have plays a very important role, because enlightenment and happiness and insight are only possible on the basis of suffering and confusion. The Buddha said it is because of the mud that the lotus can bloom. If you plant lotus on marble, the lotus cannot survive.

If you call yourself a Buddhist but your faith is not made of insight and direct experience, then your faith is something to be re-examined. Faith here is not faith in just a notion, an idea, or an image. When you look at a table, you have a notion about the table, but the table might be very different from your notion. It's very important that you get a direct experience of the table. Even if you don't have a notion of the table, you have the table. The technique is to remove all notions in order for the table to be possible as a direct experience.

We have so many wrong notions and ideas; it is dangerous to believe in them, because some day we may find out that that idea is a wrong idea, that notion is a wrong notion, that perception is a wrong perception. People live with a lot of wrong perceptions, ideas, and notions, and when they invest their life in them it is dangerous.

Let us discuss, for instance, our idea of happiness. Each of us, young or less young, has a notion of how to be happy. We believe that if we get this or that, we will be happy, and that until we realize these things, happiness is not possible. Most of us tend to have that kind of attitude.

Suppose someone asks you, "What do you believe or think to be the most basic conditions for your happiness?" They may suggest that you reflect a little bit on it and write down on a sheet of paper the basic conditions for your happiness. This is a very wonderful invitation for us to re-examine our notion of happiness. According to the teaching of the Buddha, our notion of happiness may be the obstacle to our happiness. Because of that notion, we may remain unhappy for our entire lives. This is why it is so crucial to remove that notion of happiness. Then you have the opportunity to open the door to true happiness, which already exists inside and around us.

If you are committed to one idea of happiness, then you are caught. You may not be happy all your life. You think that if your idea cannot be realized, then happiness will never be possible. That is why a notion is an obstacle. There are many ways to be happy, but you are committed in only one way. That is a loss. A young person may say, "If I can't marry that person, it's better to die because happiness cannot be possible without that person." But you don't have to die. There are other ways to be happy, but because you are only committed to one idea—that happiness is only possible with this person.

An individual or a nation may adopt an idea of happiness. Here, a group of people believes that if only their country could realize certain ideas, the whole country would be extremely happy. That idea may be a doctrine of economics or theology, or it may be an ideology. The nation believes so much in this idea of happiness that they are determined to protect and promote that idea at any cost. They would oppose any other kind of idea concerning happiness, and they would become totalitarian in their approach to happiness. There may be a government or a party which will use its strength to promote and to make that idea of happiness real. It may be that the nation has to spend seventy or one hundred years trying out that idea of happiness. During that time, they may cause a great deal of tragedy among its citizens and make them suffer so much just because they believe that this is the only way to be happy. The Soviet Union put people in psychiatric hospitals because these people didn't share the same idea of happiness. And they sacrificed a lot of people, a lot of true happiness to follow their idea of happiness.

There may be a time when a country will have to wake up from a vision of happiness, when they have to realize that theirs is not the perfect idea, that there are many aspects that do not correspond to the reality of what is there, the real need and aspirations of the people. A country might want the people to become heroes, but maybe they don't want to be heroes. The moment they release that notion of happiness, the country will again have another chance. But if people do not learn from the suffering of the past, they will repeat exactly the same mistake and adopt another notion of happiness. And we don't know how long they will keep this new notion of happiness. So a notion is always something dangerous.

The practice of Buddhism has very much to do with the removal of notions. In Buddhist practice, we aim at liberating ourselves from notions and perceptions, even notions and perceptions about our own happiness.

There is something more important than notions and perceptions, and that is our direct experience of suffering and of happiness. If our faith is made of this direct experience and insight, then it is true faith and it will never make us suffer. Last time we talked about the experience of making tofu. There are so many examples that can be used. Suppose you have learned the art of making fruitcake. You have made fruitcake several times, and because of your experience you now have faith in your capacity to make fruitcake; you are confident as far as fruitcake-making is concerned. There is only one thing that you have to bear in mind: Your art of making fruitcake can be improved. You know how to make fruitcake, but you have to be aware that there are people who are better than you at making fruitcake, and you can always improve your art of fruitcake-making.

Suppose you have suffered because of something and then you have come out of that suffering. The way you were released from that suffering may have been discovered by you, or may have been proposed to you by a teacher or by brothers or sisters. But because of your discovery, you have been able to get out of that one kind of suffering. To suffer and to know the way out of that suffering is quite a realization. You have confidence that the next time you are put in such a condition of suffering, you will know how to get out again. That is insight, that is direct experience, and they are the elements that can build up true faith.

You have learned walking meditation. You know how to walk, to dwell in the present moment, to combine your mindful breathing and your steps. You have practiced walking meditation several times and because of your practice you know that walking meditation can release you from the negative energies that make you suffer when you are upset or angry. Every time you get angry or upset or filled with despair, you practice walking meditation for half an hour or forty minutes and you always feel better. Then you know that you cannot be without walking meditation. No matter what happens to you, you will never abandon walking meditation. You also know by experience that walking meditation can be nourishing and transforming. It can bring you a lot of joy. Having faith in walking meditation is not having faith in an idea or a notion; that faith is made of direct experience. The only thing you have to bear in mind is that you can improve your art of walking, and then the fruit of walking meditation may be greater.

The same thing is true when listening to the bell, or mindful breathing, or sitting meditation. We should never say, "I have the best way of sitting," "I know the best way of walking," or "I have the best way of dealing with my anger." We know how to handle our anger, we know how to release our suffering with walking meditation, and we know how to enjoy being alive just by sitting and smiling. But we can always improve our way. Our faith is a living thing, not something static. Our faith is a living thing like a tree or an animal.

Paris is a living thing, but your idea of Paris is not. You've got an idea about Paris; you think you know about Paris. But Paris changes day and night. Even if you have visited Paris twenty times, even if you have stayed in Paris two years in a row, your idea of Paris can never be Paris-in-itself. Paris is something alive, and your notion of Paris is just like a photograph taken at a certain moment.

Faith here is a living thing, and as a living thing it has to change. We allow our faith to change. That does not mean that today I believe this, but tomorrow I will no longer believe in it and will instead believe in something completely different. A one-year-old lemon tree is a lemon tree, but a three-year-old lemon tree is also a lemon tree. True faith is always true faith, but since faith is a living thing, it must grow. If we adopt that kind of behavior and know how to handle our faith and therefore our love, it will not make people suffer.

When we believe something to be the absolute truth, we are closed. We are no longer open to the understanding and insight of other people, and this is because the object of our faith is just an idea, not a living thing. But if the object of your faith is your direct experience and your insight, then you can always be open. You can grow every day in your practice, in sharing the fruit of your practice, and in making your faith, love, and happiness grow.

There are many people who in the name of faith or love persecute countless people around them. If I believe that my notion about God, about happiness, about nirvana is perfect, I want very much to impose that notion on you. I will say that if you don't believe as I do, you will not be happy. I will do everything I can to impose my notions on you, and therefore I will destroy you. I will make you unhappy for the whole of your life. We will destroy each other in the name of faith, in the name of love, just because of the fact that the objects of our faith and of our love are not true insight, are not direct experience of suffering and of happiness; they are just notions and ideas.

Our notion of happiness is already a dangerous thing. But our notion about God is also extremely dangerous and our notion of nirvana or of Buddha may also be very dangerous. One day a Zen teacher during his Dharma talk used the word *Buddha*. He was mindful in his Dharma talk and that is why he paused a little bit and said, "I don't like to use the word Buddha; I am very allergic to that word. Dear friends, do you know something? Every time after using the word Buddha, I have to go to my bathroom and rinse my mouth at least three times." This is the language of Zen.

After the Zen teacher had declared his difficulty, a person sitting in the audience smiled, stood up, and said, "Teacher, I am also allergic to the word Buddha. Every time I hear you pronounce the word Buddha, I have to go to the river and wash my ears three times." He means, "If you are free from the notion of the Buddha, please know, teacher, that I am also free from the word Buddha and from the notion Buddha." That is the language of Zen. And through that kind of language we know that we should not be caught in words and in notions.

The word *Buddha* and the notion of *Buddha* have caused such a great deal of misunderstanding and even suffering for many people. Do you have a notion of Buddha? I am afraid that you do. Be careful. You know that three years ago you had a notion about Buddha, and now after three years of practice you have another one. This may be a better idea, but it may still be an idea.

Life is so precious, too precious to lose just because of these notions and concepts. Very often we feed ourselves only with words and notions and concepts. Please reflect. Not only do we feed ourselves with words and concepts for one, two, or three days, but we do it all our lives. Concepts like "nirvana," "Buddha," "Pure Land," "Kingdom of God," and "Jesus" are just concepts; we have to be very careful. We should not start a war and destroy people because of our concepts.

GROWING FOOD
FOR THE CHILD

~

I would like to talk to you a little bit about the Five Faculties as they are taught and practiced in the Buddhist tradition. The first is faith. We have the faculty of faith in us, and we know that faith is very important. Faith is a kind of energy that makes us truly alive. Look into the eyes of a person who doesn't have faith. You recognize at once that this person has no vitality. There is no life in him or her. If that person is animated by the energy of faith, her eyes will be shining; you can see it on her face, or in his smile. So we cannot afford to be without faith. It is a kind of energy, a kind of power.

The Five Faculties are sometimes described as the five powers. Faith is a power. With the power of faith in you, you become very active. You don't know difficulty or tiredness; you can withstand all kinds of obstacles.

Faith is the energy that brings forth the second faculty—diligence. You are active and you have energy and joy within yourself. You like to practice walking meditation and sitting meditation; you like to go to tea meditation; you like to go out and help other people to transform their suffering and to begin tasting the joy of the practice. You like to practice watering the positive seeds in your consciousness and reducing the importance of the negative seeds. Motivated by faith, you become someone truly active. When you are diligent in your practice, you develop another kind of energy within yourself called mindfulness—the third faculty.

Mindfulness has been described as the heart of Buddhist meditation. Mindfulness is to be there, alive in the present moment, body and mind united. It is the capacity of being there in order to live deeply every moment of your daily life. You are mindful when you walk, when you drink your tea, while sitting with your friends, your brother, and your teacher. You notice that the moments when you are with him or with her are precious moments. You are aware that drinking tea with the Sangha is a wonderful thing. All these things are manifestations of the presence of mindfulness. Mindfulness is to become completely alive and live deeply each moment of your daily life. Mindfulness helps you to touch the wonders of life for self-nourishment and healing. It also helps you to embrace and transform your afflictions into joy and freedom.

According to the teaching of the Buddha, life is available only in the present moment. If you are distracted, if your mind is not there with your body, then you miss your appointment with life. Mindfulness is the fruit of your practice when you have the energy of diligence within you. In fact if you are not diligent, your mindfulness cannot grow.

If mindfulness is there, another kind of energy is also there, that is the energy of concentration—the fourth faculty. When you drink your tea in mindfulness, your body and your mind are focused on just one thing, your drinking tea. When you live concentrated, you touch deeply what is there, and you begin to understand the depth of what is there. This is insight. Suppose you are there, with your body and mind in perfect harmony, and enjoy a leaf or a flower. You are not distracted. You can totally be with that leaf or flower. Since you are able to touch it deeply, to listen to it deeply, to look deeply into its nature, you begin to understand, to have a correct vision of what it is. The object of your concentration may be a flower, a person, a cloud, a child, your coffee, your bread, or anything.

That kind of understanding is called insight—the fifth of the Five Faculties. Insight is the fruit of direct experience. This flower is no longer a notion. The person I look deeply into becomes the reality, the object of my mindfulness, my concentration. She is no longer a notion or an idea. If you live with someone and you do not know much about her, then you don't live with the reality of that person—you live with your notion of that person. That is why we have said before that your faith is not made of notions and ideas but of a substance called insight or direct experience.

You have gone through your suffering, you have gone through your happiness, you have gone through your direct encounter with what is there, so with that you build your faith. Your faith cannot be taken away by anyone, it can only grow and grow and grow. When you nurture that kind of faith in yourself, you will never become a fanatical person because this is true faith and not the grasping at a notion.

If you have an idea or notion about the Buddha, you know that you can transcend that idea or notion. You must get a direct experience of the Buddha. How can you grasp the Buddha directly as a reality and not as a notion? It's easy. It's not because you have spent ten years in studying the life of the Buddha that you can grasp the reality of the Buddha. The Buddha, according to the living tradition of Buddhist meditation, is a living thing that you can experience in the here and now. The substance that makes a Buddha is awakening. Buddha means "the one who is awake."

The Buddha is not a Buddha just because he was born in such and such a place, has a particular name, is the son of a gentleman called Suddhodana and a lady called Mahamaya. Siddhartha is a Buddha because in him there is the element of enlightenment. What is enlightenment? Again, an idea about enlightenment is not enlightenment. Look into yourself, and you know that enlightenment is something you may have within yourself. When you begin to understand, when you have been able to free yourself from a notion, that is enlightenment. And you have been enlightened so many times in the past. You have entertained illusions in the past. You have suffered because of these things and when you got out of these illusions and wrong perceptions, enlightenment was born in you. Don't say that enlightenment is foreign to you. You know what it is. When you drink coffee, when you hold the hand of your child and walk, when you are really there, fully present and concentrated, you enjoy it more. You understand more of what is going on. That is mindfulness. That is concentration. That kind of mindfulness, concentration, and insight improves your happiness, your peace. That is universal. In the West, they say, "Pull yourself together and be there." You can bring these enlightenments together, help them to grow, and make them into a heritage. You can make them a base for your action, for your practice, and for your life. Then you will notice that you are extremely rich as far as spirituality is concerned.

Each one of us has suffered, of course. Out of our suffering we have learned many things, but have we profited from them? Have we gained insight?

Mindfulness is the energy that carries within itself

the energy of concentration and of insight. And each of us knows that we have mindfulness in us. When I drink tea, I can drink it in such a way that mindfulness is there. Drinking tea, I am aware that I am drinking tea; that is called mindfulness of drinking. Breathing in, I know that I am breathing in; that is mindfulness of breathing. Walking with the Sangha, I know that I am walking with the Sangha; that is mindfulness of walking. Drinking in the here and the now, being with what you drink, is mindful drinking. Breathing in the here and the now and touching deeply your in-breath and your out-breath is mindfulness of breathing. Walking in the present moment, enjoying every step you make, and enjoying the Sangha that is walking with you, that is mindfulness of walking. You know that mindfulness is not a foreign thing to you.

You do have the capacity for mindfulness, and if you practice with the Sangha, the community, for a week or two or three, you will nourish and cultivate that energy in you. That energy will become stronger and will bring you more concentration and insight, which will build your faith, love, and happiness. We always say that mindfulness and concentration are the Buddha inside of you.

You don't have to go back two thousand five hundred years in order to meet the Buddha. You sit here and touch the energy of mindfulness and concentration in you. Here you are with the Buddha; you are the Buddha. If you practice with diligence, you know that you are cultivating that precious energy within you every day, and you know that your understanding, your tolerance, your kindness, and your love depend on that energy. You know that the Buddha is not a word, the Buddha is not a notion; the Buddha is a reality that you can touch every day. And with that kind of faith in yourself, you will never become a totalitarian person. You will never try to impose your notions and ideas on others, because your faith is true faith.

GIVING BIRTH TO THE CHILD

On Christmas Eve we speak about faith, about energy, about the Holy Spirit. To me, the Holy Spirit is faith, the Holy Spirit is mindfulness; the Holy Spirit is love. The Holy Spirit is already there within us. If we are able to touch it within ourselves and help it to manifest in us, we can cultivate the Holy Spirit the way we cultivate mindfulness.

After having been baptized by John the Baptist in the Jordan River, Jesus went into the wilderness and stayed there for forty days in order to strengthen the Holy Spirit in himself. During those forty days he must have sat and walked, practicing walking meditation and sitting meditation. Unfortunately, the Gospels did not record the way he sat and the way he walked. But Jesus did sit and did walk.

At the time when John baptized him, the sky opened and the Holy Spirit came down to him like a dove and entered into him. It is so described in the Gospels. Jesus went into the wilderness in order to strengthen that energy within him. He then had the energy to perform miracles of nourishing and of healing in his public life.

The Holy Spirit is something to be cultivated, and the seeds of the Holy Spirit are already within you. To be baptized is to have the opportunity to recognize that this Spirit and that energy are already in you. To be baptized is to recognize the Holy Spirit and to touch it within you. When baptism is celebrated, the people make the sign of the cross in order to remind the congregation, the Sangha, the community, of the presence of God, God the Father, God the Son, and God the Holy Spirit.

In the moment of baptizing, the head of the person is submerged into water one, two, three times. The person who is to be baptized will be born from that water and from the Holy Spirit. In the Orthodox tradition, people like to have the whole head submerged into the waters of baptism. But in the Catholic tradition, people may prefer only to pour the blessed water over the head of the person to be baptized. That kind of ritual aims at helping people touch the seed of the Holy Spirit that is already in him or in her. This ritual is undertaken to help someone to be born in his or her spiritual life. A child is born; Jesus is born every time the Holy Spirit in you is touched.

The same thing is true for someone who practices the Dharma. Every time you touch the seed of mindfulness and mindfulness manifests in you, life is possible again. In a state of distraction, body and mind are not together. If you are lost in the future or in the past, you are not alive. But when the seed of mindfulness in you is touched, suddenly you become alive, body and spirit together. You are born again. Jesus is born again. The Buddha is born again.

When you hear the meditation bell, you stop your thinking. You stop what you are saying, and the bell rescues you and brings you back to your true home, where the Holy Spirit and mindfulness are alive.

There you are born again; you are born several times a day, thanks to the Sangha surrounding you. This is the practice of resurrection. We die so many times a day. We lose ourselves so many times a day. And thanks to the Sangha and the practice, we also come back to life several times a day. If you don't practice, then when you lose your life every day you have no chance to be reborn again. Redemption and resurrection are neither words nor objects of belief. They are our daily practice. And we practice in such a way that Buddha is born every moment of our daily life, that Jesus Christ is born every moment of our daily life—not only on Christmas day, because every day is Christmas day, every minute is a Christmas minute. The child within us is waiting each minute for us to be born again and again.

You are born in order to die again; this is the fact. If the Sangha, the church, and the teacher are not there, you are likely to die again. You may die for a long time before you have a chance to be reborn again. The Sangha is your chance, your opportunity; the Sangha is your life.

We have to make steady progress in our spiritual life. There are many people who, after having been baptized, will sin and confess, sin and confess, and sin and suffer again. Is there any progress made as a result of that process? If there is not, then we have to transform our situation. We cannot afford to let things go on and on like that. It's a tragedy, and also a comedy. We have to let our faith grow. To help our faith grow, we have to let our love grow. And because our faith and our love continue to grow, our happiness will also grow. If you are not peaceful, and happy and strong, how can you expect to help other people to be happy, and strong, and stable?

So let us sit down together as a group of brothers and sisters, as a Sangha, to practice looking deeply again into our lives and how we conduct them. We are supposed to be born already in our spiritual life. How do we take care of our life so that each time we are born we can grow stronger? If mindfulness is cultivated in our daily life, if concentration and insight are cultivated in our daily life, we become more open, more tolerant, and our faith and love grow stronger within us. And we know that without the Sangha and continuous practice, we cannot grow steadily. Instead, we will be off and on, off and on, up and down, up and down. We arrive nowhere. That is not really a spiritual life.

HELPING THE CHILD GROW

When a teacher administers to you the Three Refuges and the Five Mindfulness Trainings, he or she brings you to life. The child, the holy child, is born into you. This is only the beginning, because taking refuge is a practice that you have to continue for all your life. Taking refuge in the Buddha, the Dharma, the Sangha, embracing God the Father, God the Son, and God the Spirit is not a matter of ritual. Ritual is only one means to touch and to wake the spirit up. You have to integrate the practice into your daily life, while you are eating, while you are driving your car, while you are taking a bath, or cooking your dinner. We have to learn these things, and we can do so through various spiritual traditions.

In order to help you to strengthen the Holy Spirit in you, there is the second sacrament called Confirmation. Confirmation, why? Because the Holy Son has been born in you as a baby, but maybe it's not strong yet. You have to strengthen and cultivate the Holy Spirit in you. Jesus also strengthened the Holy Spirit within him after being baptized by John. He knew that that energy in him should be nourished and that is why he went into the wilderness.

When the bishop confers Confirmation he raises his hands over those who are receiving it, and his hand embodies the energy of the Holy Spirit. In principle, when his hand is raised in this way, the Holy Spirit must be strong in his person and in the congregation. You are the person who wants the Confirmation. You open your heart so that the Holy Spirit is strengthened in you.

The third sacrament marks the solemn moment when a person makes the promise to join another human person that he or she considers to be a life companion on the path of life and practice. This sacrament is called Holy Matrimony. Or the person may decide to join the life of the monastics and dedicate his or her life to living with this community (Sangha) in order to serve God and all living beings. This is called the sacrament of Holy Orders.

In both cases, the monastic or the layperson should, for the rest of his or her life, live in such a way that enables them to receive the energy of God in their daily life. For that purpose, they have to practice regularly the fourth sacrament: the Mass, also known as the Holy Eucharist. This sacrament is both the practice to allow the Holy Spirit to inhabit us and to remind ourselves that we should allow the Holy Spirit to always inhabit us. The Sacrament of the Eucharist is successful only when the practitioner becomes capable of living each moment of his or her daily life in the presence of God. It is like a Buddhist practitioner who is capable of dwelling in mindfulness day and night, aware of what is going on in the realms of body, feelings, perceptions, and objects of perceptions.

The last sacrament is the Sacrament of the Anointing of the Sick, to help the person to die peacefully and to prepare for a new beginning. The success of this sacrament is due to the practice of the person during his life as a Christian, and also to the aliveness of the one who performs it. The success is characterized by peace and non-fear.

But these sacraments are only received on certain occasions. In fact, you have to confirm every day, and more than that—every hour, every moment of your daily life. Drink your coffee in such a way that the Holy Spirit is strengthened in you. Cook your dinner in such a way that the Holy Spirit is strengthened in you.

Is it sufficient to go to church every Sunday? No. People seem to be very kind while in church, but as soon as they get out, it seems that all their kindness is gone. A few hours in a church cannot counterbalance the time they spend out of the church if confusion, anger, and destruction will take over.

MAKING THE CHILD STRONG

∿

We have to learn the way. In the Buddhist tradition, we learn about how our mind functions. Studies of the mind are very important in Buddhism. If you read the sutras spoken by the Buddha, you know about the Buddha's knowledge of mind. His insight as to how our mind operates is very basic for the practice of the Dharma. Mindfulness helps us to recognize every mental formation that manifests in our daily life, and mindfulness takes care of all of them, whether they are positive or negative. There is no fight in a practitioner. Practicing Buddhist meditation does not transform our person into a battlefield, the good side fighting the evil side.

Non-duality is the main characteristic of Buddhist teaching and practice. The moment you know about this form of practice, you are already more peaceful. You can embrace your suffering and your negative energies in a very tender way. We learn within Buddhism that the negative is useful in making the positive. It's like the garbage. If you know how to take care of the garbage, you will be able to make flowers and vegetables out of it. Garbage can be made into compost, and compost is essential for flowers and vegetables. So you embrace everything that is in you.

The encounter between Buddhism and Christianity that has taken place and will continue to take place in the twenty-first century is something very exciting. The coming together of practitioners in the Buddhist and Christian traditions will bring about very wonderful things, and both traditions can learn a lot from each other. As I see it, if there is a real encounter between Buddhism and Christianity, there will be a very drastic change within the Christian tradition, and the most beautiful jewels in the tradition will be able to emerge. If we can bring into Christianity the insight of interbeing and of nonduality, we will radically transform the way people look on the Christian tradition, and the valuable jewels in the Christian tradition will be rediscovered.

THE WORLD THE CHILD WILL INHABIT

❧

"Our Father in Heaven, hallowed be your name." There is another dimension of life that we may not have touched, and it is very crucial that we touch it: the dimension of the Father, the dimension of the sky, of heaven. Whether you call it nirvana or Father, it's not important. What is important is that there is another dimension that should be touched.

Let us return again to the image of the ocean. Suppose we are a wave living on the surface of the ocean. We spend all our time looking at each other as waves, and we have not been able to realize that all of us are made of water and all of us contain each other. As far as waves are concerned, there is birth and death, ups and downs, I and you. But if you are able to touch the other dimension, namely, water, you'll be free from all these notions: birth and death, I and you, up and down.

Yet the water dimension is not separate from the wave dimension. If you remove the water, there will be no waves, and if you remove the waves, there will be no water. There are two dimensions: one is waves and one is water. When we are born in our spiritual life, we are encouraged to touch the other dimension: the dimension of Father. "Our Father in Heaven, hallowed be your name." Father here is not the usual notion you have concerning father. It's not your blood father because that father would need a wife in order to engender you. He would need a job, and a house for himself, and for your mother and for you to live in, and so on. In the historical dimension, if we speak of father, we also have to speak of mother, as a couple.

The word *father* in this sense strengthens notions that we may have of father. But, in the other sense, the word *Father* points to another reality, the other dimension. So we should not be stuck to the word *Father* and the notion Father. Therefore, "Hallowed be your name" does not really mean a name, a mere name. Lao-tsu says: "The name that can be named is not the true name." Therefore we have to be careful. Nirvana means extinction of all notions.

So Father is a name that cannot be named. If you have an idea about Father, please be careful. If you are not careful, you can become a dictator. The waves are the water, but if a wave tries to understand water in terms of ups and downs, I and you, then a wave will not be able to touch water. A wave, in order to touch water, must get rid of all these notions. The wave has ups and downs, but the water is free from ups and downs. The wave believes that she has birth and death, that there is birth and the wave comes up, then the wave goes down and there is death. But water is free from all that. So if the wave is trying to understand water in those terms and notions, he will never arrive at touching water.

A teacher and his student are very careful about the word *Buddha*. We use the word *Buddha* in such a way that it helps the other to be free. We listen to the word *Buddha* in such a way that we can still remain a free person. Free from what? Free from notions, free from words. God as a Father does not need fame. Does God need to be famous? We may be thinking of God in terms of ups and downs and birth and death and I and you, and this is dangerous. "Hallowed be your name." This is a very strong teaching. We have to rid ourselves of all notions of God in order for God to be there. The Holy Spirit, the energy of God in us, is the true door. We know the Holy Spirit as energy and not as notions and words. Wherever there is attention, the Holy Spirit is there. Wherever there is understanding, the Holy Spirit is there. Wherever there is love and faith, the Holy Spirit is there. All of us are capable of recognizing the Holy Spirit when it is present.

It is the same with mindfulness. If a sister is mindful, we know that mindfulness is there. If a sister is not mindful, we know that mindfulness is not there. If a sister's eyes are brilliant because of faith and love, we know that faith and love are there. The same thing is true of the energy we call the Holy Spirit: It should be recognized not as an idea, not as a word. You and I, all of us, are capable of doing so, and then we are not bound by, or slaves to, notions and words, and we know how to cultivate the Holy Spirit.

CULTIVATING THE HOLY SPIRIT

Jesus Christ practiced the cultivation of the Holy Spirit. Confirmation, the practice of the Sacrament called the Eucharist, all of these are aiming at cultivating the Holy Spirit in you. In a Buddhist temple, every time we hear the bell, there is another chance for Confirmation, for touching, for reviving, for being born again. And that is why at Plum Village we use not only the bell, but we also use the ringing telephone and the chiming clock. The clock offers music every fifteen minutes, and we receive the Holy Spirit. We touch the Holy Spirit, the mindfulness in us. The sight of a brother walking, a sister smiling, is also an opportunity for us to be reborn again. It is possible to remain mindful most of our daily life. That is the best way to cultivate the Holy Spirit in us.

"Our Father in heaven" is the other dimension.

We have to learn to live with that dimension in our daily life. We don't wait until we die in order to get to the other dimension; that may be too late. You don't have to die in order to enter the Kingdom of God. It is better to do it now when you are fully alive. In fact, you can do it only when you are fully alive. Do you think that a wave should wait until it dies in order to become water? No. The wave is water right now, only he ignores it, and that is why he suffers so much. So the practice is to recognize that the Holy Spirit is here, God the Father is here, the other dimension is here, available: "Thy Kingdom come." In fact, the Kingdom doesn't have to come and you do not have to go to it; it is already here. There is "no coming, no going." That is the language of Buddhism.

In Buddhism, we speak of the ultimate dimension and the historical dimension. Take, for example, the historical dimension of a leaf. The leaf seems to be born in April and to die in November. The leaf seems not to be existing before the month of April, and seems to stop being after falling to the ground. That is because of our way of looking, because we don't touch the historical dimension deeply enough. If we touch the historical dimension deeply enough, we will touch the nature of no birth and no death of the leaf. A wave is also like that. If you see that the wave is there, and before it rose it was not there, and that after it stops being a wave it's no longer there, then that is because you have not lived your daily life deeply enough. You have not touched the leaf and the wave deeply enough. If you do, then you will have another insight: The leaf is also eternal, deathless. The true nature of the leaf, your true nature, is the nature of no birth and no death. Birth is a notion and death is a notion, among the other notions to be removed.

We live our day-to-day life in the historical dimension. We are a child of the Holy Spirit, a child of the Buddha, we are born from mindfulness. That is why, while living in the historical dimension, we learn to live in the ultimate dimension also. When you practice walking meditation and you are about to step on a dead leaf, step on it in such a way that you can see the nature of no birth and no death of that leaf. Don't imagine that is something you cannot do. You can do it.

If you are born as a spiritual child, your practice is to live the moments of your daily life in such a way that you can touch the other dimension, the Father. Touching the Father is your practice. In touching the Father, your fear, your suffering, will vanish. "Thy will be done on Earth as it is in Heaven." This means you have to be alive and touching both dimensions, the ultimate as well as the historical. Heaven is here on earth, and earth is there in Heaven. Wave is in the water and water is in the wave. So Heaven here does not mean a spot in space; and many of our Christian friends know that. Our Father and the Heaven where our Father is are not in a distant place situated in space; they are in our hearts. There's no difficulty in seeing this in either the Christian or Buddhist tradition. Live your daily life in such a way that you touch both dimensions.

BECOME ALIVE

"Give us this day our daily bread." Please don't worry about tomorrow or yesterday, what you need is only today. If you worry too much, you will suffer. This is the practice of living deeply the present moment. The Kingdom is not for tomorrow, the Kingdom is not a matter of the past. The Kingdom is now. We need food today. Not just bread or muesli or butter. We need to be alive in each moment. We need the kind of food that makes us alive in every moment of our life so that we can nourish our faith, our love, our solidity, and our tolerance. We desperately need that kind of food.

There are so many hungry people. Not many people want to become priests in our day, but everyone is hungry. So many people are hungry for spiritual food, there are so many hungry souls. Yet the people who are motivated by the mind of love to become monks and priests are few because we do not know how to nourish them with that kind of food. We don't believe in the process of confess and sin, off and on; we don't see it as effective. But we also do not yet have the Dharma we need. That is why we have not been able to nourish our true faith, our true love. We have grasped ideas and notions as food. That is why we have never satisfied our hunger. We always speak of eating, but we never really eat.

Even though Jesus gave us the bread, we still eat the idea. The bread that Jesus handed to you, to us, is real bread, and if you can eat real bread you have real life. But we are not able to eat real bread. We only try to eat the word *bread* or the notion of bread. Even when we are celebrating the Eucharist, we are still eating notions and ideas. "Take, my friends, this is my flesh, this is my blood." Can there be any more drastic language in order to wake you up? What could Jesus have said that is better than that? You have been eating ideas and notions, and I want you to eat real bread so that you become alive. If you come back to the present moment, fully alive, you will realize this is real bread, this piece of bread is the body of the whole cosmos.

If Christ is the body of God, which he is, then the bread he offers is also the body of the cosmos. Look deeply and you notice the sunshine in the bread, the blue sky in the bread, the cloud and the great earth in the bread. Can you tell me what is not in a piece of bread? The whole cosmos has come together in order to bring to you this piece of bread. You eat it in such a way that you become alive, truly alive. You become alive just by eating a piece of bread. While you are in Plum Village you are instructed to eat your muesli in mindfulness because you recognize that your muesli is the body of the cosmos. You eat your muesli in such a way that faith is possible, that love is possible, that awakening is possible. Whether you eat it in the meditation hall or in the kitchen, it's the same. Eat it mindfully. Eat it in the presence of God. Eat in such a way that the Holy Spirit becomes an energy within you and then the piece of bread that Jesus gives to you will stop being an idea, a notion.

Where is that piece of bread? Have the twelve

disciples eaten it all? No, it's still there. The piece of bread that Jesus offered to us is still there. We have a lot of opportunities to eat it. It may take the form of muesli, or a corn muffin, or a rice cake, but that piece of bread is still there, available in the here and now. You are invited to his table, tonight, tomorrow, and forever. You need to eat it in order to become alive again so that faith as an energy, true faith, true love, is nourished in you, and happiness becomes a reality for yourself and for many others.

We celebrate Christmas. We celebrate the birth of a child. But we have to look into ourselves. There is a child in us to be born. Our practice is to allow the child to be born every moment of our daily life. Merry Christmas! *Joyeux Nöel à vous tous!*

FOUR

SEEKING THE DHARMA BODY, THE BODY OF TRUTH

Dear friends, it is the twenty-sixth of December 1996, and we are in the New Hamlet of Plum Village.

Today I would like to elaborate a little bit more on the subject of faith. Last time we said that the object of our faith should not just be an idea, a notion. We should try our best to abide by our practice. Our faith should be built on our insight, on our direct experience.

In the Buddhist tradition we practice the three refuges: *I take refuge in the Buddha. I take refuge in the Dharma. I take refuge in the Sangha.* I always say that taking refuge is not so much a problem of belief. It is a problem of practice. It's not only that you profess your faith in the Buddha: You have to actually take refuge in the Buddha. But what is taking refuge in the Buddha? How do you do it?

When we look deeply, we see that the Three Refuges can be understood in two ways. One is the practice of seeking protection. We want to be protected. Life is full of danger; we don't know what will happen to us today or tomorrow, and that is why we have the feeling of living in insecurity. We all have the need to take refuge, to seek inner protection. Therefore, taking refuge in the Buddha means seeking security in the Buddha.

It depends on our insight and understanding of what the Buddha is and who the Buddha is as to whether our practice is deep or less deep and we can distinguish "popular Buddhism" from "deep Buddhism." These two things do not necessarily contradict each other. In the beginning, we may think that the Buddha is someone other than ourselves—another person. There are people who may think that the Buddha is a God, and there are those who know that the Buddha is a human being like us but one who has practiced and reached a very high level of enlightenment, understanding, and compassion. However, we think that person is someone that is not us, and we have to go to him for refuge: *Buddham Saranam Gacchami*. I go to the Buddha for refuge.

If you do well in that practice, some day you will come to the understanding that the Buddha is not really another person. The Buddha is within us, because the substance that makes up a Buddha is the energy of mindfulness, of understanding, and compassion. If you practice well and you listen to the Buddha, you know that you have the Buddha nature within you. You have the capacity of waking up, of being understanding and compassionate. Therefore, we have made progress and now we are seeking the Buddha from within. The Buddha ceases to be the other. The Buddha can be touched everywhere and especially within yourself. Unless you touch the nature of the Buddha or Buddhahood, you cannot touch the Buddha. If Shakyamuni, the historical Buddha, has Buddhahood, you yourself have your own Buddhahood. That is something that we have to arrive at.

In the beginning, we say, "I take refuge in the Buddha." Later on we say, "I take refuge in the Buddha within myself." That is how the Chinese, the Japanese, the Vietnamese, and the Koreans chant when they recite the Three Refuges. "I take refuge in the Buddha within myself."

"I take refuge in the Buddha, the one who shows

me the way in this life." The "one" who shows me the way in this life begins by being Shakyamuni the Enlightened One. But if you practice well, you might progress. Then you know that he is not so much another person, because you have the Buddha nature in you, and you take refuge in that nature within you. It becomes a direct experience, and the object of your faith is no longer an idea about a person named Shakyamuni, an idea about Buddhahood, an idea about Buddha nature. Now you are touching Buddha nature not as an idea but as a reality. Buddha nature is the capacity of being awake, of being mindful and concentrated and understanding. And you know very well by yourself that it is a reality that you can touch within yourself at any time.

TAKING REFUGE IN
THE BUDDHA WITHIN

We have put a new translation of the Three Refuges in *The Chanting Book of the Year 2000*: *"Taking refuge in the Buddha within, I wish that everyone will be able to recognize the nature of enlightenment within themselves, and very soon be able to produce the highest mind of enlightenment, Bodhicitta."* Taking refuge in the Buddha here means to touch the Buddha nature in you, to touch the seed of enlightenment in you, to have a direct experience of that enlightenment nature in you, so that you will produce, and open up the thought of enlightenment, the vow of enlightenment. Bodhicitta is the deepest desire in each of us, the desire to become awakened, to liberate ourselves from suffering and to help living beings.

Taking refuge in the Buddha in this way will be the practice of generating the energy of love. You see the suffering in yourself and around you and you are determined to end the suffering by touching the nature of understanding, compassion, and enlightenment in you. Because you can touch the Buddha nature in you, you produce the mind of enlightenment. You make the vow to become a Bodhisattva in order to bring relief and transformation to all living beings. It is a very powerful statement and a powerful practice. Once you are filled with the energy of Bodhicitta, you become a Bodhisattva right away.

"Producing the highest mind." Here it is said very directly that the highest mind is Bodhicitta—producing the mind of love. We know right away that this is not just a formula to recite or an attempt to seek refuge or protection. It is more than that. There is protection, of course, but this is the highest kind of protection. When you realize that you have the Buddha nature in you, when you know that the energy of the mind of love is in you, then you become a Bodhisattva and you can confront any kind of danger or difficulty.

THE DHARMA WITHIN

Taking refuge in the Dharma within, I wish for everyone to learn and master the Dharma doors, and together we engage ourselves on the path of transformation. When you really want to take refuge in the Dharma, you have to learn and to master all these teachings and practices offered by the Buddha and by the Sangha. "Together we engage ourselves on the path of transformation" means that the practice should be continued, should be taken up every day of our life, and the work of transformation should be done every day. So it is not only a matter of belief, of protection, but of practice. The Dharma is to be practiced. A mere declaration does not help very much. You have to live up to that kind of statement that you make.

THE SANGHA BODY
IS YOUR BODY

❧

Taking refuge in the Sangha within, I wish that every-
one would be able to build up the four communities,
guide, embrace, educate, and transform all living beings.
The four communities or the four Sanghas are the
Sangha of monks, nuns, laymen, and laywomen.

When you chant the Third Refuge, you know that
you have things to do. Your job is to help build the
Sangha because the Sangha is the only instrument by
which you can realize the ideal of the Buddha and
the Dharma. A true Sangha is like a vehicle trans-
porting the Buddha and the Dharma. Without the
Sangha, we cannot help living beings. We cannot do
the work of transformation in the world. Therefore,
taking refuge in the Sangha you have to actually par-
ticipate in the work of Sangha-building. You have to
use your talent to convene, to embrace, and to make
it into one solid body. It also means to educate, to
transform, and to make the Sangha more beautiful.

Now if we compare it a little bit with the ancient
translation, we see some difference. The old translation is: "When I take refuge in the Dharma within,

I vow that everyone will be able to enter deeply into the *tripitaka,* the three baskets, and their wisdom will be as large as the ocean." The new phrase is a more practical formula. When you take refuge in the Dharma, not only do you have to learn the Sutras, you have to really possess and grasp the concrete practices, the Dharma doors. And together with other people, you engage yourself on the path of understanding. It is not enough to wish that everyone will be able to enter deeply into the three baskets, which consist of the discourse and precepts given by the Buddha as well as the systematic presentation of his teachings given a century after the Buddha passed away. Now it means you can be a leader; you can unify and lead the Sangha and there is no obstacle—you can do it freely.

If you consider yourself to be a good practitioner, then Sangha-building is your job. Wherever you are, you have to put your time and energy into Sangha-building. You build the four constituents of the Sangha: fully ordained monks, fully ordained nuns, laymen, and laywomen. You bring together these four constituents, and you embrace, educate, and transform living beings.

Let us follow up on what we discussed on Christmas Day on the practice of the Five Faculties: faith, diligence, mindfulness, concentration, and insight.

Truthful to the principle, we have to seek the way to go further. The principle is set in the beginning. The object of faith should not be a mere notion, a mere concept or an idea. It should be true insight into reality, true direct experience.

So when someone says, "I believe in the Buddha. I believe in the Dharma. I believe in the Sangha," the Buddha, the Dharma, and the Sangha should not be just ideas if you really want to go far. "I believe in the nature of enlightenment that is inherent within myself" may be a statement of faith made by Buddhists. Together with that statement, that person has to practice. That person has to be able to touch and recognize the nature of enlightenment within himself or herself; otherwise, it is not a practice, it is only a statement, it is only an idea.

TRUE REFUGE, TRUE PROTECTION

But what is the nature of enlightenment? There are so many people, including Buddhists, who talk about the nature of enlightenment but who do not really know what it is—what Buddhahood is. The nature of enlightenment is what we have and what we can touch in our daily life. We know already that mind-fulness is the energy that we can generate within ourselves. During walking meditation, we are able to be mindful of every step we take. So mindful walking is what you as well as your child can do. You know that mindfulness is something real and not just an idea, and if you do well you can cultivate the en-ergy of mindfulness every day and you make it into a powerful source of energy within yourself.

Here in Plum Village we have a song saying that mindfulness is the Buddha. In generating that en-ergy, you bring the Buddha into the present moment as the energy of protection that will guide you and support you. You want protection, and what is the kind of agent that is protecting you? A notion? No, a notion is not enough to protect you. Even the notion of Buddha, the notion of God, the notion of Holy Spirit is not enough to protect you. You must have something more substantial than a notion in order for the protection to be real.

You know that mindfulness is the energy that can protect us. When you drive a car, it is mindfulness that helps you not to have an accident. When you are a manual worker in a factory, it is mindfulness that prevents an accident. When you are talking with someone, mindfulness helps you not to make the statement that will break your relationship. So mindfulness is the Buddha, the agent for protection. This is the Buddha not as a notion but as a real thing. When you touch the nature of mindfulness in you, then you know that you are grounded on a solid base.

All the Buddhas and Bodhisattvas state that you have the nature of enlightenment in you. The nature of enlightenment is the very base of your being and of your practice. If you have that, there is no reason for you to get lost. From this base, the energy of mindfulness, of concentration and of wisdom, can be born as a protecting agent. Also, you have a direction to go. If you don't have a direction to go, you are lost. You cannot be happy. To know where to go is very important. If you don't know where to go, you will suffer a lot. And this is the nature of faith as understood in the Buddha's teaching.

THE THREE REFUGES ARE FOR EVERYONE

~

When you take refuge in the Buddha, you recognize your base, the ground on which you stand, the nature of enlightenment. Second, you are protected by the energy of mindfulness, concentration, and insight. Third, you have a direction, you have faith. You know where to go. Every step brings you closer to perfect enlightenment, to solidity, to freedom. When you begin to produce the energy of enlightenment, you begin to enjoy, to enjoy these three things, the path of solidity, freedom, and joy.

There are those of us who think that the three refuges are only for beginners, but that is not true. The Three Refuges are the practice for everyone. Even if you have practiced for fifty years, you still need to continue with the practice of taking refuge. When you practice taking refuge deeply in the Buddha within, or your own capacity for enlightenment, you notice that the second and third refuges are being practiced also at the same time. There is a path (Dharma), you have taken the path, and that path is the path of understanding and compassion. There are practices for you to learn and master in order for you to succeed on the path of transformation, the transformation of your being and the collective transformation of your Sangha.

Your greater Sangha is society and other living beings because your practice not only profits the society of man and woman, but it will profit trees, animals, and minerals. That is your larger Sangha. And you know that the Sangha is also an agent of protection.

Those of us who have lived in a Sangha know so well that without a Sangha we really cannot profit enough from the teaching of the Buddha and the Dharma. The Sangha protects us, the Sangha guides us, the Sangha supports us, and we cannot be without a Sangha, like a tiger cannot be without his mountain. If a tiger leaves his mountain and goes to the lowland, he will be caught by humans and killed. A practitioner without his or her Sangha will get lost, will lose his or her practice very soon. And that is why taking refuge in the Sangha is a very crucial practice. Go back to your Sangha right away—don't wait. And help build a Sangha for your protection, for your support and guidance. This is not a statement. The Sangha is not an idea, the Sangha should be a reality. It should be the object of your building, of your practice, every day.

Taking refuge in the Dharma is the same. Without the Dharma, you get lost. I take refuge in the Dharma, I have great confidence in the Dharma. Because I have practiced the Dharma, I cannot be without the Dharma. I practice so that I and the Dharma become one. Every time you feel upset, every time you wake up in the night and feel anxious or ill at ease, every time you are overwhelmed by a feeling of despair, what do you do? The Dharma is there for you, and if you have practiced, you know that to embrace your despair, to embrace your feeling of tension or ill-being with the energy of mindfulness, is a very wonderful practice. You don't have to fight. You just practice mindful breathing and invite the energy of mindfulness to come and embrace tenderly your feeling of restlessness or despair.

Sometimes you are excited and cannot sleep and you know that you need to sleep a little bit more, for tomorrow will be a long day. You may not know what is the cause of that excitement or restlessness, but you just cannot sleep. But if you know how to practice breathing in, breathing out, inviting the Buddha to come, to embrace you and to dwell with you, then very soon mindfulness will show you the cause of your restlessness or your excitement. You don't have to do anything. "Breathing in, I know that I have unrest." Recognize your restlessness or your despair and embrace it tenderly with the energy of mindfulness, and you will know how wonderful the practice of mindfulness is. You don't fight at all against that feeling of restlessness or despair or agitation. And yet a few minutes later, or ten minutes later, that feeling may change and suddenly you recover your calm. Your calm is a seed within your consciousness, and your restlessness also is a seed stored within your consciousness. Because you know that the seed of calm and restfulness is in you, you have confidence. You just embrace the energy of restlessness and smile toward it. You know that the other seed is also in you. Suddenly you find the feeling of restlessness is gone and you are able to sleep again.

Once you have the Dharma within you, you will have the feeling of safety and security. If you have not yet learned, if you have not yet mastered the methods, you have to. You have to learn it from your teacher, from your Sangha, from your practice. When you have practiced for some time, you will have confidence in the Dharma and you will take refuge in the Dharma. The Dharma here is no longer a notion or a concept because you know the practice.

All of us here in Plum Village know that when we are upset or restless, fifteen or twenty minutes of walking meditation can restore our freshness and our confidence. Because we have practiced, we know the virtue of walking meditation. We have confidence in the Dharma and are protected by the Dharma. Learning in the Dharma, practicing in the Dharma with the guidance of the Sangha, is what we do as a practice.

TRUE FREEDOM

"I believe as a Buddhist that by looking deeply into my suffering I will be able to see the path out of suffering." This is a Buddhist statement of faith also. It is like the Three Refuges—"I take refuge in the Buddha. I take refuge in the Dharma. I take refuge in the Sangha." Looking deeply is another way of expressing your faith. I know that if I look deeply into the nature of my suffering, I will see a way out. This is the teaching of the first Dharma talk given by the Buddha—The Four Noble Truths. The First Truth is the truth about suffering, and no one can see the path unless he or she sees suffering. The path is the Fourth Truth. The First Truth is *dukkha,* suffering. The Fourth Truth is *marga,* the path leading out of the suffering.

Everyone knows that if you run away from suffering, you have no chance to find out what path you should take up in order to get out of the suffering. So our practice is to embrace suffering and look deeply into its nature. When you know and see the nature of your suffering, then the path will reveal itself to you, and you just take it.

The Second and Third Truth will depend on the First and Fourth. Among the Four Noble Truths, the First and the Fourth are the most important. The Second Truth is about the nature, the cause, and the roots of suffering. Looking into this, the path will be revealed. If you take up the path of transformation and engage yourself on that path, you will reach the

Third Truth, which is transformation, the end of suffering, namely well-being—the First Truth being ill-being. Is this a notion, an idea, or a practice?

In the beginning, we don't know why we have to suffer. We don't understand our suffering. But looking deeply we find out what has created our suffering. If we have seen this, we know how to stop, to cut the source of nutrition for suffering, and then healing will take place. Suppose your liver is giving you a lot of problems and you suffer. You look deeply into the suffering and find out that it is because in the past you have been eating or drinking in such a way that suffering could not be avoided. Then you know the path: Stop eating these things, stop drinking these things, and then healing will take place. These are not mere notions, these are the things you can directly experience. Direct experience is the object of your faith.

Mindfulness is made concrete by the practice of the precepts. Look into the Five Mindfulness Trainings and you see they are concrete descriptions of mindfulness practice. All the Five Mindfulness Trainings begin with "Aware of . . ." "Aware of the suffering caused by . . ." This is the practice of mindfulness, of looking deeply into the nature of ill-being. There is suffering in yourself and in the people around you in society. You practice looking deeply into the suffering in order to see the causes, the roots of the suffering. The Five Mindfulness Trainings are not a declaration of faith only. They are the real path of transformation and healing.

THE CONCRETE PATH OF TRAINING

Studying the Five Mindfulness Trainings, you know that if humankind abides by that practice, there will be peace, love, safety, and happiness. No matter whether you are a Buddhist or a non-Buddhist, you know that if everyone abides by the practice of the Five Mindfulness Trainings, then peace and safety and happiness must be a reality. You know that the Mindfulness Trainings are born from the teachings of the Four Noble Truths. You see the suffering. You know that you have had enough of the suffering. You don't want it anymore. You want to stop so the healing can take place.

THE FIRST MINDFULNESS TRAINING

Aware of the suffering caused by the destruction of life, I am committed to cultivating compassion

and learning ways to protect the lives of people,
animals, plants, and minerals. I am determined
not to kill, not to let others kill, and not to con-
done any act of killing in the world, in my think-
ing and in my way of life.

This is insight into the nature of ill-being and insight about the path that we should take. Looking
into this training and practicing this training, you
know that you have faith. You believe that if you
practice according to the Five Mindfulness Trainings, you will receive healing and you will receive
healing for the world. Therefore, you have a direction
in which to go, you have faith that is born from insight. Mindfulness helps you to have faith. Concentration helps you to have faith, and insight helps you
to have faith.

THE SECOND MINDFULNESS TRAINING

Aware of the suffering caused by exploitation, so-
cial injustice, stealing, and oppression, I am com-
mitted to cultivating loving-kindness and
learning ways to work for the well-being of peo-
ple, animals, plants, and minerals. I am commit-
ted to practicing generosity by sharing my time,
energy, and material resources with those who
are in real need. I am determined not to steal and

not to possess anything that should belong to others. I will respect the property of others, but I will prevent others from profiting from human suffering or the suffering of other species on Earth.

This is also insight about ill-being and the path leading to well-being. This mindfulness training should not only be practiced by individuals but by groups and by nations as well. Is your nation practicing this? Or in the name of development or growth, is your nation or are your lawmakers violating it, exploiting other nations, trying to make them into a market, monopolizing them, profiting from their manpower and natural resources in order to win the heart of their own country and its people?

The Five Mindfulness Trainings should be practiced collectively in our time for a future to be possible, and that is why you have to practice as a Sangha. A city is a Sangha and a nation is also a Sangha. Perhaps you hold a position in the City Hall or even in the Parliament. Even if you are only a writer or a teacher, you know you can take up this training; you can educate people—you can invite people to join the practice so that a future can be possible for everyone. This is taking refuge in the Sangha. You have to build a Sangha in your family.

You have to build a Sangha in your city and you have to build a Sangha in your nation in order for these mindfulness trainings to be practiced. The First Training, for instance, is the reverence for life. You try your best, but you have to invite your city and your nation to practice reverence for life.

The Third Mindfulness Training

Aware of the suffering caused by sexual miscon-duct, I am committed to cultivate responsibility and learn ways to protect the safety and integrity of individuals, couples, families, and society. I am determined not to engage in sexual relations without love and a long-term commitment. To preserve the happiness of myself and others I am determined to respect my commitments and the commitments of others. I will do everything within my power to protect children from sexual abuse and to prevent couples and families from being broken by sexual misconduct.

We should also practice this as families, cities, and as nations. We know that we have seeds of integrity, seeds of compassion, and seeds of respect in us. True love must be made of respect and reverence. The kind of love that destroys yourself and the other person, that removes self-respect and your respect for the other person, is not true love. Sexual misconduct is destroying that kind of self-respect and the respect for others.

The industry of sex is something very shameful for our society. The sex industry, the production of sounds and images that water the worst kind of seeds in us, is a shame of our civilization. Filmmakers don't help us very much in watering the beautiful seeds in us. There are so many products that day and night water the worst things in us. We expose ourselves to negative watering and we expose our children to negative watering, and this is just because many filmmakers want to make money. They pollute our consciousness and the consciousness of our children. We try to stop them. They claim they have freedom of expression. That is not freedom. That is the lack of responsibility.

In Plum Village, when you come and stay one month or three years, you have the opportunity to protect yourself from such programs. In Plum Village, we know we should not expose ourselves to television or radio programs that contain toxins. We only want to open our heart to the Dharma rain that can water the seeds of joy and hope and peace in us.

This will help the work of transformation and healing in us to take place because we know that if we
open ourselves to negative watering of unhelpful
seeds in us, then we will continue to get sick and feel
unrest. This is really taking refuge.

Taking refuge is to create an environment where
you are safe, safe from assailment or attack. We know
that our children are very vulnerable. They are being
assaulted from all sides by this kind of watering. As
a member of the city council, as a member of the
government, as a writer, as a filmmaker, as a teacher
or an educator, can you do something to protect
yourself and to protect our children? Taking up the
Five Mindfulness Trainings and protecting your society could be a great joy.

THE FOURTH MINDFULNESS TRAINING

*Aware of the suffering caused by unmindful
speech and the inability to listen to others, I am
committed to cultivating loving speech and deep
listening in order to bring joy and happiness to
others and relieve others of their suffering.
Knowing that words can create happiness or suffering, I am committed to learn to speak truth-
fully with words that inspire self-confidence, joy,*

and hope. I am determined not to spread news
that I do not know to be certain and not to criti-
cize or condemn things of which I am not sure. I
will refrain from uttering words that can cause
division or discord or that can cause the family or
the community to split apart. I will make every
effort to reconcile all conflicts however small.

"Aware of the suffering caused by unmindful speech . . ." Again, this is the practice of mindfulness and looking deeply into the nature of our suffering to see a way out. Mindful speech, loving speech, and deep listening are the path, the Fourth Noble Truth. When you make the declaration, "I believe that by looking deeply into the nature of suffering I can recognize the path leading me out of suffering," you are making a real and concrete practice.

These Five Mindfulness Trainings are the collective insight of a great many Buddhists who have practiced mindfulness. We know that many families and many couples have split up just because of the lack of practice of mindful, loving speech and deep listening. We should take up this practice and encourage this practice in the family, in the city, and in the nation. Maybe one day you will come to the Parliament and follow a debate to see how people use their speech. Are they able to listen to each other?

Are they able to convey their insight to the other, or are they just absolutely separate islands? They may only be there to fight for their preconceived ideas and not to listen and to learn from other people.

Parliaments and Congresses are places where the Fourth Precept has to be learned and practiced the most. These people are the cream; they are selected by the people of the country to represent them. If they are not able to listen to each other or to communicate with each other, how can our country have a future? How can the people of the country be understood by the government? This is an age when the Five Mindfulness Trainings should be practiced collectively by people as nations.

THE FIFTH MINDFULNESS TRAINING

Aware of the suffering caused by unmindful consumption, I am committed to cultivate good health, both physical and mental, for myself, my family, and my society by practicing mindful eating, drinking, and consuming. I am committed to ingest only items that preserve peace, well-being, and joy in my body, in my consciousness, and in the collective body and consciousness of my family and society. I am determined not to use alcohol or any other intoxicants or to ingest other items that

contain toxins such as certain television pro-
grams, magazines, books, films, and conversa-
tions. I am aware that to damage my body or my
consciousness with these poisons is to betray my
ancestors, my parents, my society, and future gen-
erations. I will work to transform violence,
anger, and confusion in myself and in society by
practicing a diet for myself and for society. I un-
derstand that a proper diet is crucial for self-
transformation and for the transformation of
society.

This very crucial practice is the hope for our future, and if we cannot practice it as a city or a nation,
we cannot transform our situation. The Five Mindfulness Trainings are a complete expression of mindfulness practice, and this mindfulness is the fruit of
our faith, of our insight, of our concentration, and of
our diligence. If we don't diligently practice looking
deeply, we cannot find out the nature of our suffering and identify the path that we need. The Buddha
always reminds us that nothing can survive without
food, our ill-being too. If we know how to cut off the
source of nutrition for our ill-being, it will have to go
away. A proper diet is what we and our society really
need. We have to prescribe that diet for ourselves
and for our society.

As we know, the second of the Five Faculties is diligence. It means diligent practice—daily practice. Because you have faith in yourself, you have the vitality in you. And because of your vitality, there is a desire, the deepest desire in you, *bodhicitta,* and that is why you are so diligent in the practice—the practice of walking, of sitting, of looking, of listening, of applying these Mindfulness Trainings in your daily life. In this way, you improve your quality of life, you transform yourself, you heal yourself, and you help the society on the path of healing, on the path of understanding and loving.

CHRISTIAN REFUGE

When we examine the Apostles' Creed or the Nicene Creed, we might find in Christianity equivalent teachings. However, we should bear in mind that there is a real danger of being caught in words, and that the object of our faith may be just notions and concepts and not true practice, not direct experience. Our Christian friends, having heard this Dharma talk, may be interested in looking again at the Apostles' Creed:

THE APOSTLES' CREED

I believe in God, the Father almighty,
creator of heaven and earth.

I believe in Jesus Christ, his only Son, our Lord,
He was conceived by the power of the Holy Spirit
and born of the Virgin Mary.
He suffered under Pontius Pilate,
was crucified, died, and buried.
He descended to the dead.
The third day he rose again.
He ascended into heaven,
and is seated at the right hand of the Father.
He shall come again to judge the living and the dead.

I believe in the Holy Spirit,
the holy Catholic Church,
the communion of saints,
the forgiveness of sins,
the resurrection of the body,
and life everlasting. Amen

The Nicene Creed says: *I believe in one God, the Father, the Almighty, maker of heaven and earth, of all that is seen and unseen.* In this statement is the intention to go back to our true home: the ultimate dimension.

It may be interesting or even helpful in these days when we celebrate Christmas to reflect a little bit on these expressions of faith.

I believe in God, the Father almighty, creator of heaven and earth. This is the equivalent of the ultimate dimension of reality, namely nirvana. The other day we spoke about waves and water. As we are initiated in our spiritual life, we should try to touch the other dimension of our being, the ultimate dimension. The wave has to touch the water in order for her fear to disappear so that she can overcome all these notions and concepts. This is a very important practice. The ultimate aim of our practice is to reach nirvana, to touch nirvana, which will bring the greatest relief.

I believe in Jesus Christ, his only Son, our Lord. In the tradition of Buddhism, the Buddha is not unique because there are so many Buddhas, countless Buddhas of the past, of the present, and of the future. But all the Buddhas embody the supreme enlightenment, the supreme compassion. And we also are future Buddhas and all of us embody the Buddha nature.

We are the waves, but we carry within us the water. We live our historical dimension, but we carry in us also the ultimate dimension. And that is why the notion *only* is not applied here. That is one difference. That does not mean that in Christianity this teaching is something foreign. Many of our Catholic, Protestant, and Orthodox friends live and know that God the Father is not out there in space but is in our hearts. The question is how to touch him or how to touch that ultimate dimension. The Sacrament of Baptism or Confirmation or the Eucharist are just ways or means to allow us to touch that ultimate dimension, to recognize it as being there. So you are invited to reflect on the word "only." *You* are also a daughter or a son of God. You are Jesus. All of us are Jesus. Every wave is born from water. Every wave has water as substance. Every wave carries within herself the dimension of water.

In Buddhism, and especially in the Northern school of Buddhism, *every one* of us has Buddha nature and *every one* of us is a Buddha-to-be. To say that you are a Buddha-to-be is to speak from a dimension called historical. But from the ultimate dimension, you are already a Buddha. The wave is already water.

THE DHARMA BODY OF JESUS

In the Buddhist tradition, whether the Buddha was born in Kapilavastu or another place is not important. Whether he was son of Suddhodana and Mahamaya is not important. Whether he was born from the side of his mother or in the usual way does not matter. Whether after his birth he took seven steps and lotuses bloomed on his steps or not does not matter. What matters is that he has offered a teaching that is available, a very concrete teaching dealing with suffering and a path out of suffering, and you can try out all these things. And through that teaching and the practice, you touch Shakyamuni Buddha as a reality and not just a concept.

It is suggested to our friends that we all go back and rediscover Jesus as a teacher. Many of our Catholic, Protestant, and Orthodox friends have that intention. They want very much to rediscover Jesus as a teacher and to learn from him the Dharma. And that is the true Jesus, the Jesus not merely as a name, as a concept, but as a living reality.

We want to discover Jesus' Dharmakaya. "Kaya" means body. We are not really interested in the body made of flesh. We are interested in his Body that is made of the Holy Spirit. We are interested in knowing his Body as teaching, because that is very crucial to us. Because that is what we want from a teacher. A teacher has a teaching to offer, and we know that if we cannot get that teaching, then we do not have the teacher. The teaching of Jesus Christ, the way proposed by him for us to get out of our suffering, is called the Teaching Body, the Dharmakaya—the Dharma Body is the teaching.

As for Shakyamuni Buddha, we know that the Dharma Body is available. We are here today in order to touch the Dharma Body of the Buddha. The Five Faculties, the Five Mindfulness Trainings, the First Truth and the Fourth Truth all belong to the Dharmakaya of the Buddha as a teacher. We take refuge in the Dharma because we need the Dharma in order to get out of our present situation of suffering. Therefore, we need the Son very much as a teacher, and more than that we need his teaching. That is not clearly presented here as the object of faith.

In the Gospels, the teaching of Jesus is clear, but in theology it may not be considered to be crucial. We want the Dharma of Jesus—please find a word for that. *I believe in the Holy Spirit and in the holy Catholic Church.* How can the Holy Spirit dwell in your daily life? Jesus Christ has proposed and has offered the practice. I don't think it is enough to say, "I believe in the Holy Spirit." It does not do justice to what Jesus Christ has taught and offered.

If we conceive of the Holy Spirit as a kind of energy that helps us to be alive, to be protected, to understand, and to love, then the Holy Spirit should be presented in concrete ways, in concrete practices as we see in the Five Mindfulness Trainings. This is something we can do and that our friends within the Christian tradition can do. Where there is the Holy Spirit there is true presence, there is true understanding, there is true communication and true love. Where those Five Mindfulness Trainings are, these qualities also exist.

HELPING BUDDHA
AND CHRIST

In the Buddhist tradition, there is the Sangha that embodies the Buddha and the Dharma. If the Sangha does not possess the true Buddha, and the true Dharma within itself, then it is not a true Sangha. If there is no harmony, if there is no practice of the Mindfulness Trainings, if there is no compassion, no insight, no happiness, that is not a true Sangha. Even if it is made of monks and nuns and laypeople, it is not a true Sangha. The form may look like a Sangha, but the content is not a Sangha because the Buddha and the Dharma can't be found in it. The same must be true of the Christian church. If there is no Father, no Son, no Holy Spirit in the Church, the Church is not the true Church. The Church has to embody the Holy Spirit, the Father, and the Son. The Church has to embody tolerance, understanding, compassion, and that is the practice of Sangha-building.

If in the Buddhist tradition every one of us has the task of Sangha-building, then in the Catholic Church, in the Protestant Church, in the Orthodox Church everyone has also the task of Church-building. Church-building does not mean just organizing. Church-building means leading your life in such a way that the Church becomes more and more tolerant, understanding, and compassionate so that every time the people go to the Church they can touch the Holy Spirit. This is an invitation for all of us because this is our practice as Buddhists and as non-Buddhists; it can be applied to every spiritual tradition.

The encounter between different traditions can help to renew every tradition. And this is what we hope for the twenty-first century. We know that peace cannot exist if religions are always in conflict with each other. If we want to stop the conflicts between religions, we have to start the dialogue between different traditions with an open attitude. We know that religion has been the cause of war in so many centuries.

Remember that the Church has been responsible for so much suffering, so much war. It is our task to build a Sangha, to build a church in such a way that the Holy Spirit, that mindfulness, should prevail so that tolerance becomes possible and understanding becomes possible in order to make compassion possible. This you practice for peace and you practice for the future of our children and grandchildren.

Let us practice breathing with the sounds of the bell.

FIVE

THE MEANING
OF LOVE

Dear Sangha, today is the twenty-ninth of December 1996, and we are in the Upper Hamlet in our Winter Retreat.

Today we continue on the subject of faith and love. We are used to saying that God is love and that we are supposed to love God with all our might. Elsewhere in the Gospels, you are told that if you don't know how to love your neighbor you are not loving God at all.

These two things have to be considered in order for us to really understand the meaning of love. The other day we spoke of the Father as the ground of being, as the ultimate dimension of reality, of life. It is very helpful for us to look back at the real meaning of these words we use; otherwise we don't really mean anything when we speak.

We know that the ultimate dimension and the historical dimension are two dimensions of the same reality, but the relationship between the two dimensions is really the problem. We know that between the waves that are seen on the ocean there is a relationship. When you contemplate all the waves on the ocean, you may find out that this wave is born because of the other waves, and looking more deeply, you see all the other waves in this wave. This is true with everything that is in the world. When we look at one flower, we know that this flower is made of all these non-flower elements, like the cloud, like the sunshine, the Earth, and so on. We see all in the one and also the one in the many. You see the relationship between things, between phenomena. All the waves have a relationship with each other. They influence each other and they make each other

But at the same time, we know that besides that kind of relationship between phenomena, there is another kind of relationship which is the relationship between the wave and the water, not the wave with other waves. It is the dimension of water and every wave is water. When we speak of this ultimate dimension, we have to be aware that our relationship with the ultimate dimension is different; it is not like our relationship with other phenomenal events around us. That is why in Buddhism there is awareness that we should deal with the ultimate dimension in a different way than the way we deal with each other in the historical dimension. On this side, we do not speak in terms of waves, we do not speak in terms of phenomena. We speak of water, we speak of the ultimate dimension or noumena.

There must be a relationship between water and waves. There is the nature *(svabhava)* and there is the appearance *(laksana)*. Waves are water, waves are somehow born from water. That is why we adopt the language that waves are sons and daughters of water. Water is the father of waves. Water is the mother of waves. It is a causal relationship. But that kind of relationship is quite different from the relationship between phenomena. If we study the phenomenal aspect of a wave, we will find out all the elements that have been converging in order to make this wave possible. Look at a person—that person is like that because their father and mother are like that, their teacher is like that, society is like that, the economic system is like that, and the culture is like that. All these elements determine the shape, the nature, the value, the happiness, and the beauty of the phenomenon called wave.

THE UMBILICAL CORDS

This wave has a father, mother, brothers, sisters, and friends. In the Buddhist language, we say that if you look around, you do not see anyone or anything that is not your father or your mother. A pebble is also your mother, a cloud is also your father. A squirrel is also your father, a deer is also a mother. That is true because there is an umbilical cord linking us with all the other phenomena around us. There is an umbilical cord joining us with the cloud. The cloud is really a mother. If we cut the cord, we have no relationship or no connection with the cloud, and then we will not survive because we know we are made of at least 70 percent water. So it is true that the cloud is our mother, and the fire is our father. We can speak of everything as our father and mother. This is a statement made by the Buddha: "Living beings are fathers and mothers for each other." We can only understand that with this kind of looking.

But when we go to the other dimension, the ultimate dimension, the dimension of the noumena, we have to be careful. We cannot mix up the water with all the waves here. There is a causal relationship, but it is quite different. That is why water should not be considered in the same way or on the same level with waves. That is what in the Buddhist tradition is called the "separate investigation of noumena and phenomena." The awareness is very clear.

When you use a word to describe something in the one dimension, it does not mean exactly the same as when you use it in the other dimension. When you use the word *father* in the historical dimension or in terms of phenomena or the wave, it does not mean the same thing as when we say *Father* in the ultimate dimension, the realm of water, or "Our Father in heaven." You have to understand it in a completely different way. This is another language.

In Buddhism there is the term—*nirvana.* It is a kind of Father. Nirvana is the kind of reality that cannot be described by notions or words. Nirvana means literally extinction, and here extinction means the extinction of notions and concepts and ideas and words—even the word *nirvana,* even the word *Father.* Therefore, with any word you use to point at the noumenal dimension you have to be careful. You should not get caught in that word. So when you say, "We should love God our Father with all our might," when you make a declaration like that, when you try to practice deeply, you have to know that that kind of language cannot be understood exactly like the kind of language we use in the realm of the historical dimension. Are you talking about loving nirvana? Does nirvana need your love? When we say God is love, is that love of God of the same nature with the kind of love you are cultivating over here in the historical dimension?

PERSON TO PERSON

Of course, every wave belongs to all the other waves. Every living being is related to every other living being. Jesus is a wave, like you and me, like the Buddha, because you can touch him as one wave in the historical dimension. We can conceive of him first as a teacher, a human being and the Son of Man. He is at the same time the Son of God.

But let us consider him and examine him as the Son of Man. As the Son of Man, he has the five el-

ements: form, feelings, perception, mental formations, and consciousness. We can touch him as a
wave, as a human being, and there is a relationship
between us and him. There is a Catholic priest who
described Jesus as our brother. During the time he
celebrated the Eucharist with me and with others, he
invoked Jesus as our brother. It means that in the
historical dimension we are brothers and sisters to
each other. We are fathers and mothers to each other
because we are all Sons and Daughters of Humankind. Then the relationship we have with Jesus is
the relationship between one person and another
person. You are making a telephone call "person to
person." *"Person to person, please."*

This person is an extraordinary person; he is a
teacher and he carries within himself the Way. "I am
the Way." And the Way is Tao. The Way is the
Dharma.

The Dharma is deep and lovely. Because the Way
and the Dharma dwell in him, he is our teacher. He
has become our teacher. Jesus is our Lord because he
embodies the way, he embodies the Dharma. There
is a kind of love between both of us. "Jesus loves me,
this I know." We know this because first of all Jesus
is the Son of Man—he is a living being. He has the
five elements, and we can conceive, we can see the

nature of love between us and him. Love your teacher, love your student. This is what we know and practice every day. We practice as a teacher, loving our students. We practice as students, loving our teacher. That is why we want to offer our teacher a cup of tea, we inquire whether our teacher is healthy, whether he can eat his breakfast, and whether he can sleep a few hours a night. We do care about his well-being, we do care about him not having too many problems and too many difficult students.

We know the nature of our love. Loving Jesus is something we can experience. We need our teacher, we need our students, and with his presence around us we feel happy. This love is quite tangible, touch-able, and conceivable.

LOVING NIRVANA

But when you say, "I love God," God here is God the Father, our ultimate dimension. We know that the kind of love we address to our Father, our heavenly Father, would not be of the same nature. When you say, "I love the Buddha," this is easy to understand because the Buddha is my teacher, he worked very hard to transmit to us his teaching and his insight. Sometimes he needed Ananda to massage his feet; sometimes he needed Sariputra to help him organize the Sangha or to help difficult students of his; sometimes he got sick, and therefore our love for the Buddha is the love of a disciple to a teacher.

But when we say, "You should love nirvana," it is quite different. It is very difficult for me to love nirvana the way I love the Buddha, or the way I love you. So we have to understand what it really means to love God or to love nirvana. Let us try to meditate together in order to get out of the words and the notions we may have been struggling with or may have been entangled in.

In the Buddhist tradition, we speak of bodies of the Buddha. It may be helpful in understanding the Trinity. The Buddha had his Nirmanakaya—the body of transformation—and it is this body that we are dealing with in our daily life. We bow to his manifested or transformed body. It is said that sometimes he manifests himself as a child, sometimes as a woman, sometimes as a businessman, and sometimes as a politician. We need to have a little bit of intelligence and vigilance in order to recognize his or her presence when he manifests himself.

It is not so difficult. Wherever and whenever there is mindfulness, true presence, compassion, and understanding, Buddha is there. You should not be fooled by the appearance. You may be facing a true Buddha, but you just ignore him or her and you do your best to run into a temple that is very far from there. You believe that going to the temple you will see the Buddha, but by doing so you are turning your back on the real Buddha. You are running after something that is not really the Buddha, or maybe a Buddha in bronze or copper, not the real living Buddha.

There is another body of the Buddha that is recommended to us. When the Buddha was about to die, he recommended to his students to touch the other body. He said that you might miss this body which is not as important as the other body of mine, which is the teaching body of a Buddha, the Dharmakaya. For us it is not too difficult to touch the Dharma body of the Buddha because although he has a physical body, he also has his Dharma body. I have my Dharma body, too, and you have also your Dharma body. It is growing, it is revealing itself with your practice. So although you have your physical body, you also have your Dharma body.

The Buddha recommended to his disciples that after his passing away physically, they should take refuge in his Dharma body which means, first of all, the body of the teachings that have been transmitted to the community of monks and nuns, to the world. The Buddha said, "My physical body is not so important; I have used it, but I have also offered you my Dharma body which is more important, and you should try to keep that Dharma body alive for your happiness." So we know that the Buddha has other kinds of body. Later on, the expression Dharma body is used in a deeper sense—it is used like the ground of being, suchness *(tathata),* or reality as it is *(bhutatathata).*

If we try to look, we will see that there are differences between our love for the Buddha and our love for his Dharma body. You love the Buddha, yes, but you love also the Dharma. Your love of the Dharma is already different. The Dharma does not need a massage, the Dharma does not need a bowl of soup, because the Dharma never gets sick. But you know that you need the Dharma, you have faith in the Dharma, you love the Dharma. The love you address to the Dharma is real, you really love the Dharma, but your love of the Dharma is not the same.

Now let us go back to the wave. The waves are supposed to love each other, because they are not enemies, because they depend on each other to be. Therefore, when a wave sees the interbeing nature of the waves, he will see that he is one with her and she is one with him. This is a wave-to-wave relationship, and with deep looking that relationship becomes very close. It has something to do with the relationship between waves and water. When a wave makes a connection, realizes the connection between her and the water, he finds also a kind of relationship which is very intimate because wave is always water. The wave does not have to die in order to become water; it is water right now, right here.

The Kingdom of God is the same; it is not situated in space and time. You do not have to die in order to enter the Kingdom of God; in fact you are already in it now and here. The only thing is that you don't know that.

Sometimes we say that God is in our hearts, the Kingdom of God is in our hearts. It means just that. But we are not truly happy when we make such a statement because we do not actually experience that. The wave may be aware that it is made of water. But the wave may be so bound to the suffering and the difficulty she is having with other waves that she is not able to realize that she is in an intimate relationship with water, and water is also the ground of all the other waves.

To love your God with all your might, what does

it mean? It is this: In your daily life, you have to seek in order to touch the other dimension of your reality, the ultimate dimension, the dimension of God, the dimension of water. It is a pity that you spend all your time dealing with the phenomenal world and becoming entangled in it without having any opportunity to go back and touch the deepest dimension of your being.

WAVES TOUCHING WATER

When you are baptized, or when you take the Three Refuges, you have an opportunity to be born as a spiritual child of your tradition. That is a kind of stimulus or opportunity for you to wake up and realize that you have a very deep need to grow spiritually.

Let us say that you would like to enroll yourself as a student at a very prestigious university. Finally you have all the qualifications and you get a student card and have access to the library, the classroom, and so on. But that is not everything, because to be in a university is to be there in order to study. After you have received The Three Refuges, after you have received

Baptism, you know that you have to continue as a child in your tradition, and therefore you have to practice in order to grow. In the Buddhist tradition, you come to a practice center and you learn how to walk and do walking meditation. You walk so that you can touch the Kingdom of God every time you touch the Earth. You walk in such a way that with every step you touch nirvana, you touch the Dharmakaya, you touch the depth of your being. When you eat, you eat in such a way that you touch the entire cosmos.

Jesus taught his disciples how to eat during the Last Supper. Eat in such a way that you can touch the body of God, the body of the cosmos. In Plum Village, at breakfast time, having some bread or some muesli, we eat our bread and our muesli in such a way that we are in touch with the body of the cosmos, nirvana—the water. You have the chance to do that all day, not just for one hour of sitting meditation or half an hour of chanting. The Sangha is there to help you; you can enjoy being there in the Kingdom of God twenty-four hours a day. You are a full-time student of that university and you are provided with a library, with books, with teachers so you can be a full-time student. So in a practice center you should be here as a full-time student not only when you practice sitting or walking but when you wash the dishes or when you make a pot of tea.

That is the true meaning of loving God with all your might. You do not reserve for that object of your love only a few minutes or one hour a day. You have to devote twenty-four hours to touching the Kingdom of God, to touching the ultimate dimension that is deep in you. You can only love your God with all your might when you are really a full-time student or practitioner.

There is another aspect of the teaching. It is not because you abandon all phenomena that you can touch the dimension of the noumena. If you throw away the historical dimension, there is no ultimate dimension for you to touch. You have to touch God through his creatures. You have to touch the ultimate dimension by touching the historical dimension deeply. If you are about to step on a dead leaf, you know that you can touch the ultimate dimension when you step on that leaf. You can touch the nature of no birth and no death of the leaf.

Living artificially, you might believe that the leaf belongs to the world of birth and death. That leaf was born in the month of March. In the month of October, it fell to the ground, and now at the end of the year, you are stepping on it. If you are not really there, if you don't live very deeply your practice, if you are not really a full-time student, you will only step on the leaf of birth and death. But if you are living deeply, then when you step on it you touch the nature of the world of no birth and no death, because birth and death are only the outer appearance.

If you touch the leaf deeply, you will see that the leaf is smiling to you, "Hello, don't think that I am dead, I am going back into the form of a leaf next April. Come back and see me in my green color."

You are also of the nature of no birth and no death, and once you have touched your nature, your true nature, all your fear will vanish. That is why you need to say that the greatest relief you can get is non-fear *(abhaya)* and that greatest relief can be obtained by touching nirvana, by touching the ultimate, by touching the Father.

How do we touch nirvana? You just touch what is there in the phenomenal world. You touch one wave deeply and you touch all the waves because the nature of the waves is the nature of interbeing, so when you touch one, you touch them all. When you chew a piece of bread, you have eternal life because the piece of bread is your whole body, and the body of the whole cosmos. The quality of eating, the quality of touching, the quality of walking depend on how concentrated you are, how present you are in the here and the now for your practice.

When you touch the ultimate dimension, you have not left the historical dimension. The relationship between wave and water is somehow linked to the relationship between wave and wave. That is why you understand the Gospel. Unless you know how to love your neighbor, you cannot love God. Before placing an offering on the altar of God, you have to reconcile with your neighbor, because reconciling with your neighbor is to reconcile with God. It means that you can only touch God through his creatures; you will not understand what is love, the love of God, unless you practice the love of humanity.

You can't touch the world of no birth and no death unless you learn how to touch the world of birth and death. That is the message of the leaf and of everything that is around you. Touching deeply the leaf or a wave or a person, you will touch the nature of the interconnectedness of everything. You will touch the nature of impermanence, of non-self, of interbeing. By touching the nature of interbeing, no self, you are touching the ultimate, you are touching God and nirvana. We have the distinction between the ultimate dimension and the historical dimension, but in fact the two dimensions are just together. There is an illusion to be removed.

THE ESSENTIAL SUFFERING

We are all tempted to go to a place where there is no suffering, where there is only peace and happiness. You may be tempted to consider that the Kingdom of Heaven is such a place, that the Pure Land is such a place. We tend to believe that there is a place where we can go by abandoning, or leaving behind, this world full of suffering, confusion, and pollution. The pollutions that afflict us are anger and hatred, despair, sorrow and fear. When you suffer so much, the tendency to want to leave it behind becomes very strong. I don't want to be here any more, I want to get out. "Stop the world, I want to get off."

Look deeply and you will touch the fact that happiness and well-being cannot be separated from suffering and ill-being. This is the interbeing nature of happiness and suffering. There is an illusion to be removed—that happiness can be without suffering, that well-being can be without ill-being, that right can be without left.

If you don't know what hunger is, you would never know the pleasant feeling of having something to eat. Do you prefer not to have any moments of being hungry at all? Or, do you prefer sometimes to be hungry in order to be able to enjoy eating some bread, some butter, some muesli? Imagine someone who is never hungry; he or she has no desire to eat at all. Why do you eat when you are not hungry? I think you like to preserve the privilege of being hungry from time to time so you may enjoy the joy of eating. If you are not thirsty, then the drinks are not appealing to you, even Coca-Cola! If you don't suffer, you would not know what happiness is.

I think we need some suffering, all of us, in order to appreciate the happiness that is available to us. You should know that breathing in and out, for many of us, is a wonderful thing. If you have an asthma crisis, if you have a stuffed-up nose, if you have a lung infection, if you are caught in a room with no fresh air, then you know the joy of being in the open air, with your lungs still in good condition, with your nose free. You enjoy walking then and breathing, in and out. Breathing in and out and walking can be very enjoyable.

To have two feet strong enough to run and walk around is also a great joy. There are times when you have a broken leg, when you have a sprained ankle, or when you are very sick. The outside seems very tempting, but you cannot get up and go out. You cannot run or walk. In these moments of suffering, you know that walking is a joy, that breathing is a joy, and just looking at the blue sky is a joy. We all need some amount of suffering in order to be able to appreciate the well-being and happiness that are available to us. You need the darkness in order to appreciate the beautiful morning.

THE KINGDOM OF HAPPINESS

Just imagine a kingdom where there is no suffering at all; it is very distressing. The joy to be alive can be there only when you know what dying is. The joy of being healthy, of being able to walk and run and breathe, will not be possible without your experience of death and sickness. Our hope, our desire, and our aspiration for a kingdom or a place where suffering does not exist should be re-examined.

The people who live in that Kingdom are not supposed to suffer at all. It seems that they should experience only happiness in their daily life. This is something absurd and impossible. A pure land, a Buddhaland, or paradise, is not a place where suffering doesn't exist. My definition of paradise is the place where love exists, where compassion exists. When the Bodhisattva of Compassion comes down to hell, hell stops being hell because the Bodhisattva brings love to it.

Yet, love cannot exist without suffering. In fact, suffering is the ground on which love is born. If you have not suffered, if you don't see the suffering of people or other living beings, you would not have love in you nor would you understand what it is to love. Without suffering, compassion, loving-kindness, tolerance, and understanding would not arise. Do you want to live in a place where there is no suffering? If you live in such a place, you will not be able to know what is love. Love is born from suffering.

You know what suffering is. You don't want to suffer, you don't want to make other people suffer, and therefore your love is born. You want to be happy and you want to bring happiness to others. That is love. When suffering is there, it helps give birth to compassion. We need to touch suffering in order for our compassion to be born and to be nourished. That is why suffering plays such an important role even down here in paradise. We are already here in some sort of a paradise surrounded by love, but there is still jealousy, hatred, anger, and suffering around us and inside of us.

It is because we are struggling to free ourselves from the grip of suffering and affliction that we learn how to love and how to take care of ourselves and of others, not to inflict on ourselves more suffering, and not to inflict on others more suffering and misunderstanding. Love is a practice and unless you know what suffering is, you are not motivated to practice compassion, love, and understanding.

I would not be willing to go to a place where there is no suffering because I know that living in such a place I would not experience love. Because I suffer, I need love. Because you suffer, you need love. Because we suffer, we know that we have to offer each other love, and love becomes a practice.

The Buddha of love, Maitreya, will never be born in a world where there is no suffering. This is the right place for the Buddha of love to be born, because suffering is the element from which we can create love. Let us not be naive and abandon this world of suffering, and hope for a place—whether we call it nirvana or the Kingdom of God or the Pure Land. You know that the element with which you can create love is our own suffering, and the suffering we experience every day around us.

PURE LOVE, PURE LAND

In the Pure Land sutra that I was translating into Vietnamese, there is a sentence that has upset me for the last many years. That sentence is: "The people who live in that Pure Land never experience suffering, they only enjoy happiness." I didn't like the sutra just because of that. But I translated the sutra because during a night when I did not sleep deeply, I heard the voice from my heart that I should translate it.

From time to time there is some sentence like that which you find in a sutra. According to the criterion of Buddhist studies, there are statements that reflect the absolute truth and there are statements which express only the relative truth. So I accept that sentence expressing the relative truth.

In the Gospel according to Matthew, there is one sentence that makes me very upset also. That sentence is found also in Mark. It is the question asked by Jesus just before he died. He called out, "My God, my God, why have you abandoned me?" "Eli, Eli, lama sabachthani." It is a very distressing sentence. If God the Son is, at the same time, connected to God the Father, why speak of abandonment? If the water is one with the wave, why complain that the water is abandoning the wave? That is why when we study the sutras or the Gospel, we have to be very awake. We should not get caught in just one word, one sentence, one statement. We have to take a broad view of the Dharma body.

I am the Way. The Way cannot be distinct from me. The Way is also me. I am the Son of God, and the Son of Man at the same time. This is very revealing and strong. Complaining that the water has abandoned the wave is something which does not reveal this same insight, this experience. Loving God, loving nirvana, loving the water means that we have to really be born in our spiritual life. It means that we have to devote all our time and our life's energy to searching for and realizing our ultimate dimension. We are thirsty, we are all thirsty for that. In order to fulfill the task of a spiritual child, we have to devote our life to touching the ultimate. We have to be a full-time student in the university. To do that you have to get into a Sangha in which everyone is doing the same; everyone is trying to be a full-time student. The Pure Land of Amita Buddha is meant to be a university where all students like to practice full-time.

In the Pure Land sutra that I translated yesterday, there was a very nice sentence. There were many nice sentences, but this one was especially nice. It says, "Dear people, when you hear me speaking of that Buddha, his land, his community, you should make it a vow to be born in that land right away. Because being born in that land you will be living together and in permanent touch with very lovely people." That means if you are born in that land you have the chance to live twenty-four hours a day with good, lovely people.

Where is the Pure Land? How can you be reborn in that land? To me, the Pure Land is here, it is in the here and the now. Each of us is Amita Buddha, because we have that energy of love, that mind of love in us, that big desire to make happiness for so many people. Each one of us has to behave like Amita Buddha, to create a Pure Land in order to provide our friends with the opportunity to live in such a safe and loving environment where everyone can practice as a full-time student. We all must have that desire, to set up a Pure Land or a practice center or a community where people can come and become one member of the community.

To be born in that community, in that Pure Land, is not difficult. You just telephone and you say, "Can I come? Do you have a room for me?"

You should have courage to leave behind all the attachments that keep you from being born in the Pure Land. When you have come to the Pure Land, you will be welcomed by the people in that Pure Land and they will encourage you to become a full-time student.

Whether you live in America, Australia, or Africa, it is your desire to set up such a Pure Land which is for the happiness of many and is a kind of university where everyone will be able to become a full-time student. With the Sangha, with the Pure Land, it is much easier to devote our time to touching the ulti-mate, because by touching the ultimate we free our-selves and make our love grow for the sake of many.

INFINITE LIGHT, INFINITE LIFE

We should be like Amita Buddha, not wishing to make the happiness of only one or two persons, but we should be more ambitious and vow to make the happiness of many people. The way to do it is to set up a Pure Land, a Pure Land in Africa, in Asia, in North America, and in South America. Your career is the career of enlightenment, of love.

Who is Amita Buddha? You should be him because Amita Buddha is a person whose light can travel very far and can reach many worlds. Listen to the definition of Amita Buddha in the Pure Land sutra:

> *Sariputra, why is that Buddha named Amita? Because he emits a lot of light, and his light can touch countless worlds around without any obstacles.*
>
> That light is the light of mindfulness, the light of love, the light of the practice.
>
> *Sariputra, why is that Buddha called Amita? Because his life span, as well as the life span of the people of his country, is limitless.*
>
> Because the practice of mindfulness, the practice of compassion, the practice of looking deeply will help us to realize and touch the world of no birth and no death. Therefore the life span is infinite.

On New Year's Day we will continue our discussion on the theme of love, because, according to the Buddhist tradition, New Year's Day is the anniversary of the Buddha-to-come: the Buddha of love.

SIX

JESUS

AND BUDDHA

AS BROTHERS

Dear friends, it is the twenty-fourth of December 1997, and we are in the Lower Hamlet of Plum Village. We are here for our Christmas Dharma Talk. First I would like to talk with you a little bit about my practice of the bell, the sound of the bell, because later tonight we are going to listen to many sounds of the bell.

SENDING YOUR HEART
ALONG WITH THE SOUND

~

When I was a small child I used to go to the village Buddhist temple with my mother, my sister, and my father. I heard the sound of the bell a lot, but it did not make very much sense to me. I remember there were people who were still talking when they heard the bell.

I became a novice monk at the age of sixteen, and at that time I had a chance to discover what role the sound of the bell really plays in the practice of Buddhism. I was given a little book to learn by heart. The book had in it about fifty-five small poems, or gathas. There were a few poems about inviting the bell to sound and about listening to the bell. It was wonderful. It was the first time I learned that the bell has a great role to play in the life of a monk and the life of a layperson.

We always say "inviting the bell to sound" since it is kinder than "hitting" or "striking the bell." Before you invite the bell to sound, you recite this poem as you breathe in and out deeply:

Body, speech, and mind in perfect oneness
I send my heart along with the sound of this bell.

May the hearers awaken from their forgetfulness
and transcend the path of all anxiety and sorrow.

When you recite one line, you breathe in. When you recite the next line, you breathe out. You recite it silently within your mind. After you have recalled these four lines of the poem, you become calm, you become solid, and now you have the right to touch the bell.

When you invite the bell to sound, you are sending your love, you are sending your greeting, you are sending your wish to the people who will hear the bell. You wish that when they hear the bell they will stop suffering; they will begin to practice mindful breathing and have the energy of peace, of joy, in themselves and will be able to transform the energy of anger, suffering, and despair in them. That is why inviting the bell and sending the sound of the bell to the people around you is a very compassionate action. You cannot do it without putting your whole heart into it.

I also memorized the poem concerning how to practice listening to the bell. When you hear the bell you are to practice deep listening:

Listening to the bell I feel the afflictions in me
begin to dissolve. My mind is calm and my body

is relaxed. A smile is born on my lips. Following
the sound of the bell I go back to the island of
Mindfulness and in the garden of my heart the
flowers of peace bloom beautifully.

We learn these poems, or gathas, by heart in order to practice listening to the bell. Inviting the bell to sound and listening to the bell can bring about the energy of peace, of joy, of solidity in you.

This evening, December twenty-fourth, we shall practice sitting meditation together. The sitting today is very special because after fifteen minutes we will begin to hear the sound of the church bells in northern Russia. We will sit very silently and we will listen to the bells of an Orthodox Church in northern Russia for about twenty minutes. We shall be sitting together silently, solidly like a mountain and free like the air. We will allow the sound of the church bell to touch the seeds of solidity and joy within us. If you do well, the seeds of joy, of love, and peace will begin to bloom like flowers in the fields of your hearts. You may have a chance to discover the true nature of the bell.

The sound of the bell in the Buddhist temple, the

sound of the bell in an Orthodox Church, in a Catholic Church, and in a Protestant Church: their nature is the same.

THE SOUL
OF ANCIENT EUROPE

In my country, I heard the Buddhist temple bells, but from time to time I also heard the Catholic Church bells. I was not really touched by a church bell. While leading mindfulness retreats in Western European countries I always asked retreatants to practice listening to church bells the way they did to Buddhist temple bells. But the first time I was touched deeply by a church bell was when I visited the city of Prague.

In the spring of 1992, we visited Moscow and Leningrad. We offered retreats and Days of Mindfulness in Russia, and then we went to other countries in Eastern Europe. We had a retreat in the city of Prague. After many days of hard work, we had a lazy day and went to visit the great city. I was walking very slowly with a number of friends and a number of monks and nuns. We were looking at the lovely postcards in a little church. The road was very small, but very beautiful.

Suddenly I heard the church bells. This time it went very deeply into me. As you know, I had been listening to church bells before, many times everywhere, in France, in Switzerland, and in many other countries. But this was the first time a church bell touched me very deeply. I felt that it was the first time I was able to touch the soul of ancient Europe. I had been in Europe for a long time. I had seen a lot. I had learned a lot about the civilization, the culture, and had met with many Europeans. Only this time, walking in the city of Prague, was I able to touch the soul of Europe in a most profound way because of the sound of a church bell.

Anything good needs time to ripen. When enough conditions come together it brings about what has been latent in us for a long time. I first came to Europe during the time of war in Vietnam. I was busy with the work of trying to end the killing. I was traveling and talking to people and holding press conferences. I was rushing around, and I did not have enough time to get into deeper contact with European culture and civilization. Prague was also not destroyed during the Second World War. It was a beautiful city that was still intact, and that is why it helped me to get in touch with the soul of Europe. Right on that spot. That sound of the church bell. It happened just like that.

When you are rooted in your own tradition you have a much better chance of understanding another tradition. It is like a tree with roots. When it is transplanted, it will be able to absorb nutrients from the new soil. A tree with hardly any roots will not be able to get the nutritious elements.

In Prague, we stood there very quietly and listened to the bell. While I listened to the bell I heard also behind it the sound of dripping water. The sound of dripping water did not come from the city of Prague. It came from a deep memory of what had happened to me when I was a young boy.

MEETING MY HERMIT

I was about eleven years old and on a small mountain in northern Vietnam called Na Son. I went up to the mountain with several hundred schoolboys and girls for a picnic. We had climbed the whole morning. Because we did not know how to practice climbing meditation, we climbed very quickly and halfway up we were exhausted and had drunk all our water and were very thirsty. I had heard that on the top of the

mountain there was a hermit who practiced to become a Buddha. I had never seen a hermit, so that
day I was very excited. I wanted to see a hermit, to
see how he practiced to become a Buddha.

Three years before that, when I was eight, I had
seen the drawing of a Buddha on a Buddhist maga-
zine. The Buddha was sitting on a spread of fresh
green grass. He looked so peaceful, so relaxed, and so
happy. I was impressed. Around me, people were not
so calm, and I had suffered from that. Looking at the
Buddha's picture, I suddenly wanted to become
someone like him, peaceful, relaxed, and happy. That
is why I was excited to meet the hermit, someone
who was practicing the way of the Buddha to become a Buddha himself. However, when we arrived
at the top of the mountain, we heard that the hermit
was not there, and I was deeply disappointed. I guess
a hermit is a man who wants to live alone and he
does not want to meet three hundred children all at
the same time. That is why he must have hidden
himself somewhere in the forest. But I did not lose
all my hope.

My group of five boys was told to take out the
food we had brought and have lunch. We no longer
had any water, but we had our rice and our sesame
seeds.

I left my friends and went alone into the forest hoping that I would be able to discover the hidden hermit. After a few minutes, I began to hear the sound of water dripping. The sound was very beautiful; it was like a piano. I followed it, and very quickly I discovered a beautiful natural well. The water was so clear, you could see everything at the bottom.

When I saw the little well I was so happy. Nobody had made that well. It was fashioned from stones and a stream of water pouring into it. The sound of the dripping water had led me into that wonderful spot. I knelt down and took the water in my two hands and drank. I had never tasted water that was so delicious. I was so thirsty.

I had read a lot of fairy tales and was very influenced by them. I believed that the hermit had transformed himself into the well in order for me to meet him privately. After having drunk the water I felt completely satisfied. I did not feel any desire whatsoever, including the desire to meet the hermit because I thought the hermit was the well.

I lay down and looked at the beautiful sky, and because I was so tired I fell into a very deep sleep. I slept so soundly that when I woke up I did not know where I was. Only after a number of seconds, did I begin to realize I was on top of the Na Son mountain. I don't think the sleep lasted very long, but it was very deep. I remembered that I had to go back down in order to meet the other four boys for lunch, so I left the well with a lot of regret. While I was walking, a sentence formed in my head. It was in French and went like this: "I have tasted the most delicious water in the world."

I did not tell the story to the other four boys because I somehow wanted to keep it secret. I had the feeling that if I told them I would lose something. I believed that I had already met the hermit.

When I was in Prague listening to the bell, I realized that behind that sound of the bell there was the sound of dripping water that I had heard when I was a young boy of eleven. I knew that the sound of the dripping water had helped me touch deeply the sound of the church bell. The sound of dripping water stands for my own spiritual tradition, the tradition that rooted me. The sound of the church bell stands for another tradition, the Christian tradition. The first helped me to get in touch with the second.

I think rootedness means a lot for dialogue. We don't want people to get uprooted from their traditions. We want them to go back. Buddhist practice may help them to go back to their own roots.

In my country we had suffered a lot because missionaries had tried to pull us out of our own traditions. They said we could only be saved by giving up our ancestral traditions, our Buddhist practices. We don't want to do the same thing to our friends.

I realized that from the time I heard the bell in Prague I began to have roots not only from my own culture but also from the culture of Europe. If you are rooted in your own culture, you may have a chance to touch deeply and become rooted in another culture as well. This is very important.

GOING BACK
TO ONE'S ROOTS

❦

I know that there are Vietnamese who have suffered a great deal in their country. They have suffered because of their families, their government, the division, and the war. They have hated everything that was called Vietnamese. They have hated their family, their ancestors, their society, their government, and their culture, because they have suffered so much. When they went to Europe or America they wanted to become purely European or purely American, leaving behind what is called Vietnamese. They were very determined not to be Vietnamese any more, to completely forget their roots. You may ask whether they have succeeded in doing so. Is it possible to forget all your roots to become something completely different? The answer is no. I have seen and met many of them after many years of trying to be someone other than themselves. They do not succeed, and I encourage them to go back to their roots.

Thirty years of sharing the Dharma in the West has brought opportunities for me to meet Europeans and Americans who bear very much the same kinds of wounds and desires. Because they have suffered so much they want to have nothing to do with their family, their church, their society, and their culture. They want to become someone else, they want to be Indian or Chinese or they want to become Vietnamese. They want to become a Buddhist because they have hated everything relating to their roots. Have they succeeded in leaving everything behind in order to become something completely new? The answer is no.

When these people come to Plum Village, for instance, I recognize them right away. I recognize them right away as wandering souls or hungry souls. Yes, they are very hungry. They are hungry for something beautiful to believe in, for something good to believe in. They are hungry for something true to believe in. They want to leave behind everything that belongs to their society and culture.

True love needs patience. If you really want to help, you have to be patient. I know that in order to help these people we have to be very patient. My tendency is to tell them that a person without roots cannot be a happy person. You have to go back to your roots. You have to go back to your family. You have to go back to your culture. You have to go back to your church. However, that is exactly what they don't want to do, and they often become angry when we try to tell them so.

A tree without roots cannot survive. A person without roots cannot survive either. So I have to be very patient. I say, "Welcome. Practice sitting meditation. Practice walking meditation. You have the right to love the Buddha, to love the Vietnamese culture." And we try to offer the Sangha, the community, as a family to him or her. We try to embrace him or her in our practice of mindfulness, like the damp soil embracing the cutting of a plant, giving it a chance to put forth a few tiny roots. Slowly, slowly they recover a little bit of their confidence, their faith, and their capacity to accept love.

To be able to help a hungry soul, you have first to earn his or her trust, because hungry souls are suspicious of everything. They have not seen anything truly beautiful, good, and true. And they suspect you and what you want to offer. They are hungry, but they do not have the capacity to receive and to ingest, even if you have the right food to offer them, even if you have something beautiful, true, and good to offer them.

In Asia, we have a tradition of offering food and drink to wandering souls on the afternoon of the full moon day of the seventh lunar month. Wandering souls do not have a home to come back to. Every house has an ancestors' altar. Our ancestors have a home to come back to, but the hungry ghosts *(pretas)* do not. So we make an offering in the front yard of our house. The hungry ghosts are described as beings whose belly is as big as a drum but whose throats are as tiny as a needle. So their capacity to receive food or help is very limited. Even if people have real understanding and love to offer, they're still suspicious. That is why you have to be patient. That is why in the beginning of the offering ceremony we have to recite the teaching of the Buddha so the wandering souls can touch the compassion and understanding of the Buddhas and Bodhisattvas and have a chance to be reborn into the Pure Land.

In our time, society is organized in such a way that we create thousands of hungry ghosts every day. They are mostly young people. Look around us. There are so many. They have no roots. They are hungry. They suffer. We have to be careful in our daily life, trying not to help create more hungry ghosts. We have to play our role as parents, teachers, friends, and priests with understanding and compassion. We have to help hungry ghosts to be less hungry, to go back to their family and tradition, to be reintegrated.

When the time is right, when they are capable of smiling and forgiving, we tell them, "Go back to your own culture, go back to your own family, go back to your own church. They need you. They need you to help renew themselves and no longer alienate their young people. Do that not only for your own generation but for the future generations as well."

EATING EACH OTHER

Dear friends, I would like to tell you a little bit about my happiness. I am very happy every time I touch the beauty of life around me. Sometimes I feel deeply moved because there are so many beautiful things around me and also inside me. Sometimes the trees are so beautiful, the sky is so clear. Sometimes the river is so magnificent and also the sunrise, the sunset, the birds, the deer, the squirrels, the children.

There are people capable of loving, forgiving, and taking care of other people. I see people capable of loving other people and taking care of animals, taking care of the trees, the water, the air, and the minerals. I am inspired by the beauty around me and by the capacity for loving around me.

That does not mean that I do not suffer. I would also like to tell you a little bit about my suffering. I suffer a lot when I see we have to eat each other in order to remain alive. Animals have to eat each other in order to remain alive. That is a very heartbreaking fact. Of course you have observed nature yourself. You have seen films of nature. You have seen that a lion has to kill deer and other animals in order to feed herself and her children. You know that big fish eat small fish. The birds eat fish.

In the winter there are hunters around. In the distant past, people had to hunt in order to eat and survive. But now I don't think that we are starving to that point. We don't have to go and hunt any more. And yet there are so many hunters around. Every Sunday they terrorize the little creatures living around them.

If love exists, there are other things that exist also. There is ignorance, there is violence, there is craving. Humankind suffers because many of us make other people suffer. We have created war a little bit everywhere. We want to consume so much and because of this we have created a lot of suffering for each other. It is a privilege for many of us to be able to be vegetarian. I know that vegetables are living things also, they suffer when we eat them. But their suffering does not compare with the suffering of other living beings. It is not as intense.

Last Sunday I shared formal lunch with the monks and nuns and laypeople in the Upper Hamlet. I was eating my lunch very mindfully and I looked very deeply into the rice, beans, and tofu that I was eating. I saw many things in the food I ate. I saw the mud, the soil, the minerals, and the compost. I saw the rotten bones of small living beings. In order for the rice and the vegetables to grow, they need these elements. When I was eating the rice, beans, tofu, and tomato, I saw very clearly the elements that made the rice, beans, and tofu. I saw them very deeply and still the food tasted good.

Brothers and sisters who were in the Sangha surrounded me. I was aware that it was wonderful to be able to eat lunch in the presence of a practicing community. You have to eat in such a way that love, peace, and stability are possible, that you are a support to others. We have to eat in such a way that compassion is nourished within our hearts. We practice love and compassion while walking, while sitting, and while eating.

Let me invite the bell to sound and we shall practice breathing together one minute before I continue. Sit beautifully and receive the sound of the bell. Make it possible for the energy of peace to be born in each of us.

Listen, Listen, the sound of the bell
brings me back to my true home.

FINDING FAMILY

According to tradition, on Christmas Day you have to go back to your family. When I look into Christmas deeply, I realize that Christmas is very close to the spirit of the Vietnamese New Year, because in our tradition you have to go back to your family before the New Year starts.

When we come together as a family we have a chance to touch our roots deeply. We should learn to make use of this opportunity in order to be deeply present for each other and to reconcile with each other, because that is the best way to touch our ancestors. A person cannot be a happy person if he or she has no roots. Christmas is an opportunity for us to sit down, to look deeply, and to become aware of our roots. We have more stability and peace and joy if we can be firmly rooted in our own ancestors and in our own culture.

You have to be a family again. You have to touch your roots deeply again, and it is easier for you to touch your roots if every member of the family is there. That is one of the wonderful things about Christmas—that everyone is urged to go back to his or her family on Christmas Day. I hope that this practice lasts for a long time.

EMBRACING OUR SPIRITUAL ANCESTORS

We have blood ancestors but we also have spiritual ancestors. If you were born in the West there is a big chance you are a child of Jesus and that you have Jesus as your ancestor. Jesus is one of the many spiritual ancestors of Europeans. You may not consider yourself a Christian, but that does not prevent Jesus from being one of your spiritual ancestors because your great-grandfather might have been a good Christian. He has transmitted to you the seed, the energy, the love, and the insight of Jesus. If you do well, you will be able to help this energy to manifest within yourself.

There are those who think that they don't have anything to do with Christianity. They hate Christianity. They want to leave Christianity behind, but in the body and spirit of these people Jesus may be very present and very real. The energy, the insight, and the love of Jesus may be hiding in them. It is like the sound of the bell. When you hear the sound of a church bell or the sound of a Buddhist temple bell, you may not feel anything. You may think the sound of the bell has not much to do with you, but one day it may be very different.

A Buddhist is someone who considers the Buddha as one of his spiritual ancestors. You can say that the Buddha is an enlightened one, a great Bodhisattva, a teacher, and the founder of Buddhism. You can say that the Buddha is your spiritual ancestor. To me the Buddha is very real. I can touch him at any time I want. I can profit from his energy and insight any time I want. It is very real. He is in every cell of my body. Every time I need him I have ways to call for him and to make his energy manifest.

I do the same with my father. I know that my father is in me. My father is in every cell of my body. In me there are many healthy cells of my father. He lived more than ninety years. Every time I need him, I can always call upon him to help. I get his energy from every cell of my body.

I live in constant touch with my ancestors whether they are blood ancestors or spiritual ancestors. If you are a Buddhist, you have the Buddha as an ancestor. The energy, the insight, and the love of the Buddha have been transmitted to you by your teacher, and by many generations of teachers. You know how to touch these cells within your body and in your soul; you know how to make the energy of the Buddha manifest. You need the energy of the Buddha.

EMBRACING
NEGATIVE ENERGIES

Sometimes we are overwhelmed by the energy of hate, of anger, of despair. We forget that in us there are other kinds of energy that can manifest also. If we know how to practice, we can bring back the energy of insight, of love, and of hope in order to embrace the energy of fear, of despair, and of anger. Our ancestors are capable of negating the unwholesome energies, or what Christians might call the evil spirit within us, by bringing back the Holy Spirit in order for us to heal and to be healthy and joyful and alive again.

In Buddhism, we also talk about these kinds of energies, the negative energies and the positive energies. There is a little difference though. In the case of Buddhism, we don't have to chase the evil spirit away; in fact we embrace the evil spirit, the energy of anger, the energy of despair, the energy of hate, the negative energies. Embraced by the energy of mindfulness, they are transformed. They don't need to be chased away.

What do you do in order to embrace and transform them? You have to call in to yourself, you have to help manifest the energy of love, of understanding, and of peace in order to embrace these kinds of negative energies. Listening to the bell, for instance, is one of the wonderful ways to generate the energy of peace, to generate the energy of mindfulness. These energies will help to take care of the negative energies. For instance, when you are angry you can always practice like this:

Breathing in, I know the energy of anger is in me.
Breathing out, I embrace my anger.

It is a wonderful practice. You just practice breathing in and out to be aware that anger is in you. You know that when you are angry it is not good to say anything. It is not good to react or do anything. "Breathing in, breathing out, I recognize there is anger in me" is the best thing to do. If you know how to do it, the energy of anger will not be able to harm you or the people around you.

During this practice, the energy of mindfulness is in you, alive, because you continue the practice of mindful breathing in and mindful breathing out. Mindful breathing helps the energy of mindfulness to be alive, and this enables you to embrace the energy of anger, to recognize it as existing. You are put in a very safe situation. You don't have to chase anger out of you. You allow it to be in you, you embrace it tenderly, and then anger will subside, and the danger is overcome. During the practice you have helped anger, and it will be transformed slowly. This practice enables you to acknowledge your anger with a smile.

While you practice breathing in and out, acknowledging your anger and smiling toward it, the energy of the Buddha is in you. The Buddha is in you, the Buddha as an ancestor is protecting you. You know that the Buddha is not an idea. The Buddha is true energy. The energy of the Buddha is the energy of mindfulness, the energy of peace, the energy of concentration and wisdom.

If you are a Christian, your practice should be similar. When the evil spirit is within you, the spirit of despair, anger, violence, and hatred, you have to be aware that it is in you. You ask Jesus to come and to become manifest within you in order for you to be able to recognize the negative in yourself and to embrace it. With prayer and contemplation, with the reading of the Bible, you put yourself in a safe situation. You are able to contain, to control, to transform the negative energy in you, the energy you call the evil spirit. The Holy Spirit is the energy that you need in order to embrace and take care of the negative energy in you. For those of us who practice mindfulness, we believe that the energy of mindfulness (which is the energy of the Buddha) is the equivalent of what our friends call the Holy Spirit.

The Holy Spirit is the kind of energy that is capable of being there, of understanding, of accepting, of loving, and of healing. If you agree that the Holy Spirit has the power to be present, to understand, to heal, to love, if you agree about this, then you have to say it is the same thing as the energy of mindfulness. Where mindfulness is, there is true presence. Where mindfulness is, there is the capacity to understand. You have the capacity to accept, to become compassionate, to love, and therefore to touch the energy of mindfulness so that it may become manifest in you. The Buddha as a spiritual ancestor is manifest in you. You are able to allow the Holy Spirit to be in you, to guide you, to shine on you like a lamp. Jesus is then alive in you that very moment.

It is possible to know the Buddha and at the same time know Jesus. There are people who have roots within both the Buddhist tradition and the Christian tradition. In my hermitage, I put a lot of Buddha statues on my altar, about ten or fifteen very small Buddhas one centimeter high and larger ones too. I also have a statue of Jesus as my ancestor. I have adopted Jesus Christ as one of my spiritual ancestors.

During the Vietnam War I worked very hard in order to stop the killing. When I was in Europe and in North America I met with a number of Christians who really embodied the spirit of love, of under-standing, of peace, of Jesus. Thanks to these people I have touched deeply Jesus as a spiritual teacher, a spiritual ancestor.

THE MEETING
OF TWO BROTHERS

There is a filmmaker living in Sweden who wanted to come and ask me this question: "If Jesus and Buddha met today what do you think they would tell each other?" I am going to offer you my answer.

Not only have they met today, but they met yesterday, they met last night, and they will meet tomorrow. They are always in me and they are very peaceful and united with each other. There is no conflict at all between the Buddha and the Christ in me. They are real brothers, they are real sisters within me. This is part of the answer.

A Christian is a child of Jesus, having Jesus as a parent, as an ancestor. As we are children of our ancestors, we are the continuation of our ancestors. A Christian is a continuation of Jesus Christ: He *is* Jesus Christ, and she *is* Jesus Christ. That is how I see things, this is how I see people. A Buddhist is a child of the Buddha, he is, and she is, a continuation of the Buddha. She *is* the Buddha, he *is* the Buddha. You are the child of your mother. You are the continuation of your mother. You are your mother, your mother is yourself. You are the child of your father. It means that you are the continuation of your father. You are your father, whether you like it or not. You are only the continuation of your mother and your father.

So it is true to say that when the Buddhist meets the Christian, the Buddha is meeting Jesus. They do it every day. In Europe, in America, in Asia, Buddha and Christ are meeting each other every day. What do they tell each other? Imagine three hundred years ago when Jesus came to Vietnam. Do you think that the Buddha in Vietnam would have said, "Who are you? What are you here for? The Vietnamese people already have a spiritual tradition. Do you want the Vietnamese to reject Buddhism and to embrace another faith?" Would you imagine that Jesus would say to Buddha, "Well, you Vietnamese people, you follow a wrong spiritual path. You have to reject all that and you have to learn a new spiritual path that I am going to offer to you. It is the only path that offers salvation."

If you are a historian, if you have researched the history of religion, you would know what the Buddha would have said to Jesus three hundred years ago and what Jesus would have told Buddha three hundred years ago. Imagine the same meeting today in Europe and in America. But you don't have to imagine, for it is happening every day. The Buddha comes to Europe and America every day. The Buddha is saying to Jesus, "I am new to this land. Do you think I should stay here or should I go back to Asia?"

There are so many refugees who come from Indochina. There are also people coming from Thailand, from Burma, from Tibet. They have brought their religious beliefs with them to Europe and to America. Do they have the right to continue their practice here in the land of Europe? Do they have the right to share their beliefs and practices with non-Buddhists? Can you imagine that Jesus would tell them, "No, in Europe we already have Christianity, and it is not nice for you to try to propagate a new faith in this land." We can imagine all kinds of proposals, we can imagine all kinds of reactions.

Once I was in Lille, a city in northern France. In a discourse given in French I said that I could see the Buddha and Jesus sitting and having tea together. Then, Buddha turned to Jesus and said, "My dear brother, is it too difficult to continue in this time of ours? Is it more difficult to be straightforward, to be fearless, to help people to understand and to love than it was in the old time?" That could be a question by Buddha to Jesus.

In the old time, Jesus was a very fearless person, a straightforward person. He was a teacher who had a great capacity for loving, for healing, and for forgiving. The first question addressed to him by the Buddha might be, "My dear brother Jesus, is it much more difficult in our time?" After having asked that question, Buddha might continue, "What can I do to help you, my brother?" How should we design the practice so it will be understood, accepted, and effective, in order to rebuild what has been shattered, to restore what has been lost: faith, courage, and love?

Jesus is all of us in the Orthodox Church, the Catholic Church, in the Protestant Churches, in the Anglican Churches trying to help people to understand, to accept, to live, and to practice so that love and acceptance become possible again. Jesus is all these people who are concerned how the Christian message can be received easily and be understood easily today.

The question the Buddha asks Jesus is very practical.

The Buddha asks Jesus the question about practice because he wants to know the answer. At this very time, it is also difficult for him, as well, to do the things he did twenty-five hundred years ago in India. In his own tradition, people talk a little too much about the teaching. People have gone astray by inventing too many things and organizing too much. They lose the true essence of the Dharma. They are teaching and practicing in archaic forms that could not transmit the true teaching to new generations.

While the Buddha asks Jesus that question, he is asking himself that very same question: How do we renew Buddhism as a spiritual tradition? How can the Buddhist embody the true spirit of the Dharma? How can the practice generate the true energy of love, of compassion, of understanding?

The question addressed to Jesus is the question addressed to the Buddha within himself. Buddha and Jesus are two brothers who have to help each other. Buddhism does need help. Christianity does need help, not for the sake of Buddhism, not for the sake of Christianity, but for the sake of humankind and for the sake of other species on Earth. We live in a time when individualism prevails. We live in a time when violence prevails, in a time when ignorance is overwhelming. People are no longer capable of understanding each other, of talking and communicating with each other. We live in a time when destruction is everywhere and many are on the verge of despair. That is why the Buddha should be helped. That is why Jesus should be helped.

So instead of discriminating against each other, the Buddha and Jesus have to come together every day, every morning, every afternoon, every evening in order to be true brothers. Their meeting is the hope for the world.

The Buddha and Jesus have to meet every moment in each of us. Each of us in our daily practice needs to touch the spirit of the Buddha and the spirit of Jesus so that they manifest. These energies are so crucial for us to embrace our fear, our despair, and our anxiety.

It is possible, according to Jesus and according to

the Buddha, that we can restore our peace. We can restore our hope. This peace and solidity, that hope, is for those we love, for those who live all around us. Every step you make in the direction of peace, every smile that you produce, and every loving look that you have inspires and helps the people around you to have faith in the future.

That is why the Buddha should help Jesus to restore himself completely. Jesus should also help the Buddha restore himself completely because Jesus and the Buddha are not merely concepts, they are around us, alive. You can touch them in your daily life.

THE MARRIAGE OF BUDDHA AND JESUS

In many countries, including Vietnam, China, Korea, and Thailand, young people find it difficult to marry each other if they have different religious beliefs. If a Buddhist young man falls in love with a Catholic young lady, they will have a difficult time, because both families will try to prevent them from getting married. This tragedy has been dragging on for a long time. It might take one hundred years to settle the problem and to allow the young people belonging to different spiritual traditions to marry each other without suffering. But it is still a worthwhile endeavor, because much suffering will be avoided for a long time.

When two people from different traditions marry, the young man could make a vow to learn and practice the spiritual tradition of the young woman, and the young woman could make a vow to learn and practice that of the young man. In that case, both of them would have two roots instead of one, and this can only enrich each person. When they have a family, the children should be raised in such a way that they can appreciate the best things in both traditions. The parents should encourage their children to have two roots and to have both the Buddha and Jesus within their life. Why not?

This will open up a new age where people are more tolerant, where more people can see the beauty and value of other traditions. It is just like cooking. If you love French cooking, it does not mean that you are forbidden to love Chinese cooking. If it takes one hundred years to arrive at this agreement, it is still very worthwhile. If you can arrive at this conclusion, the younger generation will not have to suffer like the people in my generation and in previous generations. You love the apple; yes, you are authorized to love the apple, but no one prevents you from also loving the mango.

Thich Nhat Hanh has lived an extraordinary life in an extraordinary time. Since the age of sixteen he has been a Buddhist monk, living the life of an ascetic and a seeker of the way. He has survived persecution, three wars, and more than thirty years of exile. He is the master of a temple in Vietnam whose lineage goes back over two thousand years and, indeed, is traceable to Buddha himself. The author of more than one hundred books of poetry, fiction, and philosophy, Thich Nhat Hanh has founded universities and social service organizations, and rescued boat people; he led the Vietnamese Buddhist delegation at the Paris Peace Talks and was nominated for the Nobel Peace Prize by the Reverend Martin Luther King, Jr. He makes his home in France and Vermont.